SAVE AMERICA!

SAVE AMERICA!

H. EDWARD ROWE

Fleming H. Revell Company
Old Tappan, New Jersey

Library of Congress Cataloging in Publication Data

Rowe, H Edward.
    Save America!

    1. Christianity—United States. 2. United States—Moral conditions. 3. Church and social problems—United States. I. Title.
BR526.R68   209'.73   · 76-3517
ISBN 0-8007-0798-2

TO *my father and my mother,*
who shaped my early life
and guided me into paths
of service
for God and man

Contents

PART III   THE PROGRAM

CONCLUSION   LET US CROSS OVER

Preface

Unprecedented social, economic, and political convulsions have seized our national community. Loss of confidence in government and in public leadership at all levels is everywhere in evidence. A pervading mood of hopelessness and despair is infecting the ranks of even the most devout Christians.

Because they are convinced the devil has gained control of things, Christian citizens too frequently shrink from active leadership roles in public affairs. Many of those who profess faith in God are living as if God were dead. Their lethargy and inaction in the face of overspreading evils lends credibility to the general awareness that the walls of our civilization are crumbling in upon us.

This volume is an attempt to strike a note of hope. It is the purpose of this book to convince Christians that they can be used of God to turn the tide, and to suggest constructive guidelines for the kind of effective Christian action which can bring this about. It is released to the public in the hope that it may stimulate further Bible study, research, thought, prayer, and dedicated action to the end that the deterioration of our civilization may be arrested and reversed in our generation.

It would be impossible to assign proper credit to all who

11

have contributed to the shaping of my viewpoint as expressed in these pages. I am especially indebted to Dr. Howard E. Kershner who has for a full decade articulated privately to me, as well as publicly, the distilled wisdom of a long life of dedicated service for the betterment of mankind. R. J. Rushdoony, untiring Christian scholar and unwavering advocate of Christian application in society, has stimulated a deeper interest in many of the themes touched upon in this volume.

Dr. John F. Walvoord and the faculty of Dallas Theological Seminary led me into a deeper appreciation of the Scriptures. Dr. Carl F. H. Henry first made me aware of the fact that my relationship with the Lord Jesus Christ obligates me to assume civic responsibilities. Robert M. Metcalf, Jr., founder of the Christian Studies Center of Memphis, has underscored the urgent need for a more adequate Christian approach to economic and social problems. Dr. Francis Schaeffer of *L'Abri* has enlarged my awareness of the wholeness of biblical Revelation and its relevance to the solution of human problems.

My wife, Lois, deserves special thanks for her moral support and practical assistance during the several months which were devoted to the preparation of this book while carrying a full schedule of administrative and editorial responsibility.

Finally, many other friends throughout the nation have challenged me to seek more pertinent and effective forms of service for Christ and our country, as the shadows of spiritual and moral decay lengthen across the land. I am grateful to God for all who have conveyed their deepening concern about the problems confronting America and who have joined with me in the grand quest for solutions.

                                                    H. EDWARD ROWE

Foreword

If we are to save our nation and the whole of civilization from destruction, millions of Christians must respond positively to the challenge of this book. Few messages are more urgently needed. I wish I had written this book myself, for in a very real sense it is an expression of my own growing concern for our country and the world.

For more than twenty-five years I have been voicing the prayerful hope that a great spiritual awakening will reverse the tide of materialistic atheism that is engulfing the world. I have been praying that we as a nation will not move beyond the point of no return in our current plunge toward self-destruction through spiritual and moral decay.

We Christians must get involved in politics and government as an act of obedience to the Lord. God's servants have been admonished to "subdue the earth" (*see* Genesis 1:28). We are not to be passive spectators; we are called to be involved in the action. First-century Christians were world-changers for Christ. Whether or not we become involved in the affairs of our nation at this critical moment in history will, in my judgment, determine life or death for America.

By background and experience H. Edward Rowe is uniquely equipped to write on the urgent need for Christians to do the will of God in the life and leadership of America. He combines a thorough education, pastoral experience, a long-standing interest in national affairs, a gift of language, and other attributes which qualify him to convey the relevancy of the Scriptures to the local community and the broad national scene as well.

I commend this new book for its vigorous advocacy of Christian participation in the affairs of our nation at all major levels of influence—the home, the church, education, the media, entertainment, and government. If enough Christians will read and heed the message contained in these pages, America will soon be on the road to recovery of its great heritage of God-guided government and legislation—and as we celebrate our Bicentennial we shall experience a new birth of faith and freedom. A new day will dawn for the cause of Christ.

Every person with any degree of authority in America— the pastor, the educator, the communicator, and the public official especially—should read this book.

As you read, ask God what He would have you do *now* to help restore our nation to its Christian heritage, so that integrity, righteousness, and morality will once again be the norm in America. Remember, God blesses and uses individuals. You are important to God, and to the out-working of His great plan. Don't wait for others to act. Assume your God-given rights and responsibilities today—for the glory of God, and for the salvation of our nation and the world.

BILL BRIGHT, Founder-President
Campus Crusade for Christ
Arrowhead Springs, California

The time for action is at hand. Christians must proceed with Spirit-wrought determination to develop the programs which will effectively influence the life of our nation in the years ahead. It has happened in former times, and it can happen today.

You Christians are the salt of the earth. All the affairs of men are flavored by your presence. Without your life-preserving qualities, what hope would there be? Civilization would collapse.

Spoken by our Lord Jesus Christ in
Matthew 5:13 (Paraphrased by H. Edward Rowe)

1

Introduction: The Will of God and Citizenship

God has spoken, and we are responsible to act consistently with His directives. His Word is for our good. We must relate it faithfully to the whole range of the issues of life.

An unprecedented new movement is stirring in our nation. It is a movement inspired by the Word of God. It is motivated by mounting Christian determination to engage in effective action designed to counteract the disorders which afflict our civilization. It is a movement which expresses itself in love, compassion, outrage, indignation, and a mounting volume of appropriate action in a time which bears the unmistakable marks of spiritual, moral, social, political, and economic decline.

More and more Christian citizens are realizing that biblical knowledge implies responsibility to engage in consistent action. There is a new awareness that Christian responsibility is not fulfilled adequately through mere church attendance, moral living, and occasional ministries of personal evangelism. Commendable as these forms of worship and service are, they do not fulfill all Christian obligation. Larger

numbers of Christians than ever are finding concrete ways
to express their faith by exerting an influence in the life of
the local and national community.

A PURIFYING FORCE

Dynamic Christian evangelism has brought about a rapid
growth of the Christian community in recent decades. But
in spite of its growth, the Christian community is not making
the constructive impact on our society which it should.
Evidence of this failure is seen in the rising crime rate, the
failure of justice in our courts, the proliferation of pornographic literature and films, the secularization of our educational system, the enfeeblement of our economy, corruption
in government, and general moral decay.

Today's young Americans are being inundated with propaganda which derides a Christian moral code and encourages
free sex, condones use of the "pill" by unmarried coeds,
advocates abortion, and demands the legalization of mari-
juana. This radicalism is prevalent on America's college and
university campuses. Revolutionary student groups, pornographers for profit, and radical college professors promote
this life-style.

The rapid growth of our Christian community and the
relentless deterioration of our American society are both
happening at the same time—and these two factors are incon-
sistent with each other. A growing Christian community
should result in the increasing betterment of our people and
of our society.

The time has come for Christian Americans to move as a
purifying force in the life of the nation. Churches and Christians everywhere must proclaim the Gospel and instruct
believers with renewed vigor and unwavering steadfastness.

But evangelism and Bible teaching must not be regarded as substitutes for the performance of good works throughout all of the institutions and structures of our society. We have been ". . . created in Christ Jesus for good works . . ." (Ephesians 2:10).

ACTING IN THE WILL OF GOD

The only reliable and enduring foundation of civilization and human well-being is the revealed will of God. A fundamental purpose of Christian individuals and institutions alike should be to discover and apply the will of God for the guidance and well-being of man. The will of God is revealed in the Word of God, which is the infallible guide for the life of man on this planet. God has spoken, and man is responsible to act consistently with His directives. Divinely revealed principles are for the good of man, and they must result in appropriate human action related to the full range of human experience.

Our responsibility extends beyond the doctrinal and personal dimensions of life. Christian interest, vision, and action should fulfill the will of God in all areas of life. To be "doers of the word" (James 1:22) involves more than going to church, paying one's taxes, and living an exemplary personal life. It involves going into action to apply the time-tested truths of the Word of God in all areas of human life, thought, and activity. God commanded our first parents to "subdue" the earth (Genesis 1:28). This divine mandate is still in effect. It has far-reaching implications, extending to theology, philosophy, economics, politics, technology, the social sciences, jurisprudence, education, commerce, communications, and all other areas of human activity. To satisfy the demands of the Word of God, the Christian must be dedicated to the implementation of the will of God not only in the life of the individual, the family, and the church, but in all other areas of life as well.

CHRISTIANS MUST MOVE DECISIVELY

The Word of God clearly declares that the material dimensions of human well-being can only arise when sound spiritual principles underlie the thought, ideology, and actions of men. "But seek first His kingdom and His righteousness;" said Jesus, "and all these things [material benefits] shall be added to you" (Matthew 6:33). Only when the thoughts and actions of men are rooted in the realm of the Spirit can they produce good government, good business, good education, and a good society.

The discerning Christian repudiates the basic error of all anti-God ideologies—the error that man is capable of self-improvement apart from God. Such humanistic self-confidence can only produce anarchy, totalitarianism, mass slavery, and the general deterioration of a civilization. Unguided and unrestrained by Christian ethical and moral principles, positive evils will follow even from the political freedom enjoyed in a democratic republic and the economic freedoms allowed within a free-enterprise system—and these precious freedoms will be placed in jeopardy.

Whether he realizes it or not, every Christian in America is a part of our political system. This is true in the nature of the case, because of our democratic political institutions. Christians have no choice as to whether they should be involved in our political system—they already *are* involved. Political and civic disinterest—lethargy and inactivity on the part of Christians—is actually a form of negative involvement which promotes the ascendancy and rule of evil men. This is contrary to the will of God. "For the scepter of wickedness shall not rest upon the land of the righteous; That the righteous may not put forth their hands to do wrong" (Psalms 125:3).

For too long Christians have demonstrated an almost complete lack of interest in government. No significant number of them are becoming candidates for public office or working hard to enable good candidates to gain office. In the few instances in which Christians have gained public office, they are not adequately undergirded during their term of public service by members of the Christian community.

Because of their assumption that politics is "dirty," too many Christians have retreated from the field of public leadership. As a matter of fact, politics is no dirtier than other forms of activity. An evil person is bound to be "dirty" in whatever vocation he chooses. The great John Calvin regarded political life as one of the noblest callings of God.

Today, our most capable thought leaders are sounding the alarm. The noticeable and rapid deterioration of our civilization is taking place in our time. If our country is to be saved from a whirlwind of destruction brought about by evil forces within, Christian citizens must move decisively into the forefront of public leadership at all levels as rapidly as possible. Only they are equipped spiritually and morally to render the kind of public and political decisions which will be pleasing to God and which will lead to the strengthening of the fiber of our nation and civilization. The perspective of the Word of God must be brought to the analysis of the issues confronting our country, to the evaluation of candidates for public office, and to the open discussion and proper understanding of legislative measures.

THERE ARE CHRISTIAN ANSWERS

The rapidity with which our country's problems have piled one on top of another during the past decade has left us in a state of bewilderment. Our confidence in the legendary Yankee know-how has gone down into rapid decline. Many factional leaders have stepped forward with panaceas, most of which history has long ago tried and rejected.

But there are answers—real answers—and we Christians are the ones to whom they have been entrusted. Why then are these known Christian solutions to so many of our problems not a part of our local and national policies? The answer is that although there are enough Christians to lead our nation back to righteousness, we have no strategy for using our God-empowered influence for good. We have lost by default to secular forces whose standards of conduct invariably lead to chaos.

Such diverse personalities as Ralph Nader and Madalyn Murray O'Hair have proved that the old saying "You can't beat City Hall" is nothing but a defeatist crutch. They pursued their goals with singular resolve and made a huge impact. If consumer advocates and atheists can have their way in the life of the nation, why can't Christians?

Desperately needed are imaginative new methods for the application of Christianity in the local community. Every Christian is responsible to help build a bridge of constructive service to the community. Although the problems are national in scope, the solution must take place locally.

Every pastor and church has an obligation to offer leadership in dealing with neighborhood problems in a constructive Christian manner. Invariably such an effort will augment the spiritual ministry of the pastor. It will open doors to the community, attract people to Christ, and extend a wholesome influence for righteousness. Christians everywhere today have a unique opportunity to experience the joy and fulfillment which comes from serving Christ by applying Christianity in the community. This neglected area of Christian service—so vitally needed today—can impart new meaning to our national motto IN GOD WE TRUST. More importantly, it can usher in a new era of obedience to the will of God in our civic life.

TIME FOR CONSTRUCTIVE ACTION

I have confidence in God's ability to uplift and ennoble the whole man—spiritually, intellectually, psychologically, socially, and morally—through the redemptive work of our Lord Jesus Christ. I am convinced that God can improve man personally, corporately, communally, institutionally, and nationally. This improvement is rooted in personal appropriation of the crucified and risen Savior, which marks the beginning of a new relationship wherein the people of God are responsible to be constructively active in harmony with the eternal purpose of God, for the accomplishment of the work of God in this world. As this God-directed Christian activity occurs, the problems of our society will be solved and progress will be made toward the realization of the higher way of life which God desires for the inhabitants of planet earth.

TIMELY CHRISTIAN PURPOSE

Christian purpose today should comprehend the need to effect constructive change in American communities, and in the nation as a whole, by means of consistent application of biblical principles for the guidance of local and national affairs.

Christians must call this nation and its citizens to repentance for the sin of complacency and apathy in the face of growing evils, which threaten the very foundations of civilization.

If my people, which are called by my name, humble themselves, and pray, and seek my face, and turn from their wicked ways; then I will hear from heaven, and will forgive their sin, and will heal their land.

2 Chronicles 7:14 KJV

Alas, sinful nation, People weighed down with iniquity, Offspring of evildoers, Sons who act corruptly! They have abandoned the Lord, They have despised the Holy One of Israel, They have turned away from Him.

Isaiah 1:4

Righteousness exalts a nation, But sin is a disgrace to any people.

Proverbs 14:34

Christians must seek to introduce citizens to spiritual salvation through faith in our Lord Jesus Christ.

For He made Him who knew no sin to be sin on our behalf, that we might become the righteousness of God in Him . . . . and He died for all, that they who live should no longer live for themselves, but for Him who died and rose again on their behalf. Therefore if any man is in Christ, he is a new creature; the old things passed away; behold, new things have come.

2 Corinthians 5:21, 15, 17

Christians must be actively engaged in developing Christian leadership capable of directing responsible Christian action adequate to cope with vital issues confronting our communities and our nation.

> For the wicked shall not rule the godly, lest the godly be forced to do wrong.
>
> Psalms 125:3 LB

> And let us not lose heart in doing good, for in due time we shall reap if we do not grow weary. So then, while we have opportunity, let us do good to all men . . . .
>
> Galatians 6:9, 10

THE NEED

The need behind this statement of Christian purpose is suggested by the prevailing state of affairs in our country at the present time. We are suffering as a nation from spiritual, ideological, moral, economic, political, and social ills, which are eating at the vitals of our civilization and threaten to consume us. Identifiable spiritual and theological ills include defection from biblical faith and a strong tendency toward imbalance between personal piety in Christian living on the one hand, and responsible Christian living in the larger arena of life on the other. Humanism, secularism, and relativism are dominant in the prominent ideologies of the day. In the realm of morals, existentialism and hedonism are now woven into the fabric of our society.

The trend away from traditional moral values is evident in the home, in the media, in the school, in business, and in government. Economic ills like unchecked waste, government-induced monetary inflation, unbalanced budgets, deficit spending, and controls by the heavy hand of the bureaucracy are reminiscent of past ages marked by the decline of nations. Political corruption (which already existed) has suddenly become visible. This has resulted in confusion and mass disillusionment on the part of the public. Unwieldy and wasteful bureaucracy moves in to regulate more and more the life of the citizen, making serious inroads on his freedom and self-determination. Crime, class struggle, injustice, poverty, and pollution are among the social ills which beset us. So serious is our national sin and sickness that any enduring change can only be brought about through a determined application of guiding principles derived from the Word of God.

PURPOSE OF THIS BOOK

It is the purpose of this book to inform, motivate, and encourage all who share the high goal of bringing the revealed purpose of God to bear on those areas of human concern which are crucial to the future of our country and our civilization. The enormity of the task before us is apparent. Nevertheless, the time is at hand when Christians must proceed with Spirit-wrought determination to develop and implement the concepts and programs which will effectively influence the life of our nation for the better in the years ahead. It has happened in former times, and it can happen today.

Christian-motivated citizens everywhere are invited to share their ideas and contribute their energies in this noble partnership of righteousness—for the glory of God and for the good of our friends and neighbors throughout the nation and the world.

OUTLINE OF THIS BOOK

In the chapters which follow we will first have a candid look at the many-sided *problems* confronting our country today—the dismal trend of affairs in religious, philosophical, political, social, and cultural matters; the entrenched philosophy of God-rejecting humanism, and the pervasive presence of confusion on vital issues, even among Christians.

Proceeding to the second section, we will assess our Christian resources in terms of the *people* who can—if committed to God for this purpose—be largely instrumental in changing the direction of our rapidly declining civilization.

Finally, Part Three will set forth the *program* of strategic action whereby God-directed change can be wrought throughout the institutions of our society, beginning at the center of power.

PART I

The Problem

The outlook for the future is bleak, to say the least. Godless men are running the country while men of God rest in peace or—at the most—complain mildly. The modern mind is fashioning a new Dark Age without God, while Christians refuse to get their hands dirty with the mundane affairs of this world. The barbarians of our time are a mighty secular force working among us to undercut the pillars of stable society. They are storming the bastions of our civilization. Many of our most prominent thinkers are convinced that the great clock of history is approaching midnight in the Western world.

2

Christianity and the Trend
of Our Time

*The deeper reason for everything that is now happening lies
in the circumstance that vast, cavernous hollows were
formed in the European part of mankind by the vanishing
Christian belief, and into these everything is tumbling down.*
*Written by Vassili Rozanov during the
Russian revolution, which claimed his life*

When Neil Armstrong planted the first human footprint on
the moon on July 20, 1969, he spoke of that achievement
as a "giant leap for mankind." The incident epitomized the
advance of rationality and of order—the progress of science,
the triumph of technology.

In November of the same year that man reached the moon,
Eldridge Cleaver wrote his introduction to Jerry Rubin's
book *Do it!* He described the American national scene as
he saw it. He observed that ". . . the children are screaming
for Amerika's death." Cleaver's statement, and the 244 pages
of Marxism, nihilism, and obscenity which follow it, represent a totally different and conflicting attitude of our time—

the spirit of reaction against traditional values, against science, and against rational thought.

Looking out from the surface of the moon through the eyes of Neil Armstrong, mankind beheld a beautiful world in the distance. But from the surface of this beautiful world, a generation of ungrateful rebels could see nothing but ugliness—nothing in our culture worth saving. Everything needed to be destroyed. "Burn the flag!" roared Rubin. "Burn the churches! Burn! Burn! Burn!"

After the trials were over, the champions of violence received less press. Other convulsions like the Watergate scandals, the energy crunch, ecological choices, women's liberation stole the headlines. As the leadership level of American society repudiates God (to a large degree), history rushes at us with a mounting momentum of ills and woes. The destructive forces within our society increase and persist, in spite of a parallel increase in the numerical strength of the Christian community.

THE RETREAT FROM REALITY

The mass rejection of God brings in its wake a mass retreat from reality. Typical of the sentiment behind this retreat is a bumper sticker which displays the message STAMP OUT REALITY. A surprisingly large segment of our population—including too many evangelical Christians—have joined the Cop-out Generation.

The social and economic fruits of the philosophy of unreality are everywhere apparent. Drugs, astrology, sexual exhibitionism, witchcraft, grotesque forms of music, philosophical and religious defection, child rebellion—these are just a few of the perversions which have resulted, because thousands of our citizens have chosen the path of unreality.

The drug culture has shown its true face in the Manson murders. Everybody who knew him remarked that Charles Manson was a "nice guy"—a very likable person. Yet this representative of the drug culture and of the cult of unreason was capable of committing one of the most outrageous crimes in the annals of our country.

Another mark of the disciples of unreality is the new interest in astrology. There are thousands of practicing astrologers in the United States. A degraded theatrical performance sees a bright new world in the coming "Age of Aquarius." Magazine articles and books on witchcraft are multiplying at a rapid rate. The signs of the zodiac are familiar to the younger generation. Even professing Christians manifest varying degrees of confidence in the rule of the stars.

In the field of music there are grotesque new expressions. On the philosophical front existentialism, hedonism, and nihilism, the philosophies of relativism, of the priority of pleasure and of the destruction of time-tested values enjoy wide acceptance in our educational institutions. The ideology of Marxism, which has already seized a large portion of the world, is a major motivating force behind many of the so-called revolutionary movements. Hundreds of our universities have become incubators of Marxist revolutionary activities.

In religion, the results of European rationalism and of the denial of biblical truth are evident. The established Church in all too many instances has become a joke in the eyes of many sincere people who are in search of spiritual reality. Extremist reactions of various types have startled decent citizens. The nation is treated to the spectacle of an operating and thriving "Church of Satan," and also to new churches of homosexuals.

A QUESTION OF SURVIVAL

It has been more than a quarter century since Winston Churchill declared that the outcome of World War II would determine nothing less than the survival of what he called "Christian civilization." The inclusion of the word *Christian* in Churchill's statement betrayed his profound grasp of the fact that the cultural fountains of the West are at base theological. The Jewish philosopher Will Herberg showed his agreement with Churchill when he introduced an article entitled "Modern Man in a Metaphysical Wasteland" with the following words: "The problem of the social order is a problem that in essence is theological and metaphysical. It is the theological and metaphysical tradition that has provided the sustaining armature of Western culture."

In this same article Herberg discussed the crisis of our time. The underlying cause of this crisis, he asserts, is the fact that "the spiritual armature of our culture . . . has reached an advanced state of disintegration." And he explained: "We are surrounded on all sides by the wreckage of our great intellectual tradition. In this kind of spiritual chaos, neither freedom nor order is possible. Instead of freedom, we have the all-engulfing whirl of pleasure and power; instead of order, we have the jungle wilderness of normlessness and self-indulgence" (Intercollegiate Review, vol. 5, no. 2, Winter 1968–69).

Modern man proceeds to dispense with the divine guidelines for his life on earth. He attempts to solve his problems apart from God. His motivating philosophy springs from the Garden of Eden and is best summarized in the words of Satan to Eve: "Indeed, has God said, 'You shall not eat from any tree of the garden'?" (Genesis 3:1). Man's basic and most profound error is that he places a question mark over the Word of God.

This generation is not unlike that of the Prophet Jeremiah. Pronouncing the judgment of God on that evil age, Jeremiah thundered: "For My people have committed two evils: They have forsaken Me, The fountain of living waters, To hew for themselves cisterns, Broken cisterns, That can hold no water" (Jeremiah 2:13).

MISUSE OF TECHNOLOGY

Too frequently modern man has misconstrued and misused technology. When viewed in its proper perspective and consecrated to the service of God and mankind, technology represents a great blessing. The Christian recognizes that technology is made possible by the physical laws of nature which God has created. It is a primary tool for the fulfillment of the commission to "subdue the earth" (Genesis 1:28). It is useful in enabling man to cope with the harsh realities of nature, and to shape his environment for comfort and progress. But in the hands of men who have declared their independence from God, technology has assumed an unwarranted arrogance. Does man have a problem? Well, technology can solve it. There is no need to look to God. Technology has brought with it a mechanistic bias. It has depersonalized both God and man. In the esteem of its most ardent champions, technology has made God a lot smaller and man a lot bigger.

Marshall McLuhan, the world-renowned communications expert, has presented a vivid picture of the misuse of technology. He points to the pathetic spectacle of the children of the TV generation trying to read a book. They hold their books about six and a half inches from their eyes, ". . . striving to carry over to the printed page the all-involving sensory mandate of the TV image" (*Understanding Media: The Extensions of Man*). McLuhan goes on to show how the television screen generates in children "an urge toward involvement in depth that makes all the remote visualized goals of usual culture seem not only unreal but irrelevant, and not only irrelevant but anemic." McLuhan further comments, "It is the total involvement in all-inclusive *nowness* that occurs in young lives via TV's mosaic image." It should be clear that technology, divorced from the Creator-God who made it possible, can readily become a curse and not a blessing.

INADEQUACY OF REASON

Well, if *technology* can mislead us—what about *reason?* Plato once stated that a rejection of reason is a rejection of freedom. But reason, divorced from God, is no more reliable as a guide for man than is technology when divorced from God. Reason is a very poor substitute for Divine Revelation. The reasoning powers of the enlightened humanists of history have too frequently led mankind down the blind alleys —sometimes to destruction and doom.

As the curtain went up on the fourth decade of this century, Adolf Hitler was a man widely acclaimed in Germany for his reasoning powers. Hundreds and thousands of educators, professionals, and other intellectuals came under the spell of Hitler's reasoning powers. They often repeated a well-worn cliché of that time: "Hitler is the only one who is saying anything that makes sense these days." The greatest tyrants of history have frequently been the people with the greatest reasoning powers.

With all due respect to Plato, the experience of freedom is bound up in respect for eternal truth rather than in devotion to the faulty processes of human reason. Eternal truth comes from God. It is reality. It is the retreat from the truth of God—the truth which underlies the stability of institutions and the greatness of nations—that has sped the process of decay within our civilization. Truthlessness is the certain road to doom.

Neither technology nor reason can redeem a civilization which has cast itself off from Almighty God. Without God, reason becomes an unreliable compass, and technology soon becomes a monster. A civilization that turns away from God invites anarchy, and if anarchy shall succeed, tyranny and enslavement of the masses will surely follow. "The wicked shall be turned into hell, and all the nations that forget God" (Psalms 9:17 KJV).

APATHY RATHER THAN ACTION

In the seventeenth chapter of his *Decline and Fall of the Roman Empire*, the noted historian Edward Gibbon listed seven factors which eventually accounted for the downfall of ancient Rome. The factors were: the widespread discontent of the populace; the decline of genius and manly virtue; the rage of tyranny; the general relaxation of discipline; the increase of taxes; the threatening tempest of barbarians; and corruption in government—often taking the form of violation of the laws by the powerful. These were the death pangs of a once-great civilization.

Today, two thousand years after the death phase of the iron empire of Rome, these same factors of decline are everywhere apparent in Western civilization. For masses of people, life has lost its meaning and purpose. There is a pervading sense of hopelessness. In art and drama there is an unwholesome emphasis on the grotesque, the irrational, and the obscene. In education, secular humanism is at the helm and a disengagement of the intellect from God is taking place. To an increasingly alarming degree, education is passing under state control—a situation which can only accelerate the development of the philosophy of centralized authority.

In family life, the home is in a near-fatal crisis. The crumbling of justice is apparent in our courts. In law enforcement there is a mood of helplessness as crime rates rise on a steep upward curve.

> By any measurement, crime has become an ominous national problem. Since 1961 the rate for all serious crimes has more than doubled. From 1973 to 1974 it jumped 17%—the largest increase in the 44 years that national statistics have been collected.
>
> Violent crime has had an even sharper increase. In the past 14 years, the rate of robberies has increased 255%, forcible rape 143%, aggravated assault 153% and murder 106%.
>   "The Crime Wave," *Time* Magazine, June 30, 1975

In morals, a climate of relativism, situation ethics, and the quest for selfish pleasure prevails. In economics, the picture is dismal—deficit spending, spiraling inflation, debasement of our currency, increasing federal controls, and skyrocketing taxes.

> The evidences of decadence stab us daily: Violent crime has skyrocketed 174% in the past decade. Divorce doubles, with a million marriages expected to be dissolved this year. One in eleven Americans is an alcoholic. Eye-popping political scandals surface from the White House to the county courthouse. Suicide, drug use, pornography, filmed sex and violence, corporate price fixing, labor union corruption, misuse of church funds, a harlots' convention in a prominent Protestant church, and on and on ad nauseum.
>   JAMES C. HEFLEY, *America*
>   *—One Nation Under God*

In the field of science, humanism has gone to seed in the concept of control by a technological elite, as depicted by

B. F. Skinner (*Beyond Freedom and Dignity*), Alvin Toffler (*Future Shock*), Albert Rosenfeld (*The Second Genesis*), and others. In government, the order of the day is burgeoning bureaucracy, overspreading corruption, mass disillusionment, and loss of confidence in the institutions of power.

In theology, which has been referred to as "the queen of the sciences," there are three conspicuous trends. First, religion without revelation. This trend has appeared in this century in the form of humanistic liberal rationalism which denies that the Bible is the Word of God and arrives at religious conclusions through the rational processes of the human mind. Second, there is the trend toward occult expressions. This is apparent in the upsurge of satanic supernaturalism—the mass revival of superstition, parapsychology, astrology, spiritism, occultism.

In the third place, there is a noticeable trend toward Christianity without application. Millions of sincere Christians have been caught up in a certain pietistic withdrawal from reality. For them, Christianity is pretty much an individual and personal matter. The Bible is studied for the personal enjoyment which it brings, rather than for the purpose of discovering its applicability and doing something about it. Apathy prevails where action is needed.

BLEAK OUTLOOK—BRIGHT HOPE

Norman O. Brown exclaims, "Today even the survival of humanity is a utopian hope." In his book *Building the City of Man,* W. Warren Wagar sees twentieth-century man as "a baby in a wicker basket, wailing on the doorstep of doomsday." In the midst of the dark, the secular mind sees a glimmer of hope in historian Arnold Toynbee's prediction of an emerging world government which, he concedes, will have to be dictatorial. The outlook for modern man and the humanistic society, which he has created, is bleak.

But Christians must not fall into the trap of evaluating the trend of our time from a merely human perspective. We must align ourselves with the divine perspective—and if we do we will find that the outlook for the future is bright. We must live in the light of the reality and power of the risen, living Christ. In the darkest hour of man, God is on the throne of the universe. Man's failure is God's opportunity.

Men of faith must always see a brighter future. Almighty God has graciously declared His will through the pages of the Holy Scriptures. As in every dark hour of history, He wants to move through His people. As soon as the Christian citizens of our nation are ready to exchange lip service for life service in carrying out the will of God at all levels of leadership and influence, God will move decisively to work miracles on behalf of this nation. With God, all things are possible. With God, there is bright hope in the midst of the most dismal outlook.

THE ROAD BACK

The road back to prosperity, strength, and vitality for America lies in the direction of a return to God, the eternal Author of all truth and reality. We must seek out again "the fountain of living waters" and drink deeply of the wisdom of heaven. We must dispense with the hypocrisy of recognizing God only in our national anthem, on our currency, and in our salute to the flag. We must see Almighty God as the author and sole dispenser of true freedom. We must look to Him as the mainspring of truth and righteousness. We must seek His guidance in all areas of the life of our nation. We must recognize Him as the source of all economic, social, and political justice.

The Latin words over the podium in the California Assembly Chamber translate as follows: *It is the duty of the Legislature to make just laws.* But what is the criterion of *Justice?* The only stable and enduring criterion is the moral law of God. "Blessed is the nation whose God is the Lord" (Psalms 33:12). We must turn to the God of our fathers individually, institutionally, and nationally—if we are to find our way out of the jungle in which we are lost, and if we are to avoid a midnight of unspeakable tragedy for our civilization.

Let us not be deceived. While we rejoice with Neil Armstrong and those who have followed him to the moon, let us not worship at the shrine of technology. And let us not fall into the trap of the secular humanists, who elevate human reason to the place of supremacy. Technology and reason have allowed the soul of our people to languish—and in the resultant vacuum a whirlwind which threatens our nation is raging.

It's time to turn back to the fountainhead of our civilization. The road back to true greatness for our country is a road paved with the eternal truth of Almighty God. If this truth is to be made effective in the life of our nation, it must be applied consistently and with increasing effectiveness for the solution of our problems. The development of Christian leadership to provide new directions for America must be a top-priority goal of all people of faith who want our country's destiny to be guided by the hand of Almighty God.

In the next chapter we will begin to think about a philosophy of approach to the solution of human problems. We shall see that there are only two basic approaches—the one which originates with God, and the one which is derived from man.

3

The Two Ways:
Christianity and Humanism

Humanism is man in rebellion against the authority of God. The only adequate counterforce is genuine Christianity.

There are only two movements in history—God's and man's.

God's movement has been revealed in the Holy Scriptures, which tell us about salvation through Christ, freedom, morality, justice, and the life of service. It is theocentric: God is at the center.

Man's movement is humanism. It is based on the denial of God's existence. It is anthropocentric: Man is at the center.

God's movement is God working for man—saving and uplifting him. Man's movement is man working for man—downgrading and corrupting him, in spite of good intentions.

The Bible teaches that God has given us the spiritual wisdom on which we may build a healthy and useful life, organization, or nation.

Humanism assumes that man knows best. It brushes aside the wisdom of God. It depends on human thought processes

42

for the solution of all problems. Having cut itself off from the only reliable source of light and wisdom, it always leads men to confusion and darkness.

Humanism is the godless, groundless secular religion which underlies the warped and dangerous thinking behind much of the social activism of our time. It is satanic in origin. It represents man's effort to solve his problems and shape his society apart from God. It is exactly the opposite of true Christianity, which seeks the guidance of the Word of God for the solution of human problems.

HUMANIST MANIFESTO OF 1933

The official creed of humanism was until recently expressed in the *Humanist Manifesto*, which was published in *The New Humanist* in 1933. This document boldly denied the creatorship of God, stating that man has "emerged as the result of a continuous process." Man's religious culture and civilization are the product of "a gradual development due to his interaction with his natural environment and with his social heritage." Modern science ". . . makes unacceptable any supernatural or cosmic guarantees of human values."

According to the *Manifesto*, the time has passed for belief in God. The purpose of man's life is "the complete realization of human personality." All associations and institutions "exist for the fulfillment of human life." A better life for man can only be found through "a socialized and cooperative economic order," which must be established "to the end that the equitable distribution of the means of life" will be assured. Humanists, says the *Manifesto*, "demand a shared life in a shared world."

HEART OF HUMANISM

Since this so-called *Manifesto* first appeared in 1933, various intellectual humanists have become increasingly aware of its inadequacy. Paul Blanshard, author of the book *American Freedom and Catholic Power*, is a humanist thought leader and contributor to the pages of *The Humanist*. In 1973 he took part in a forum sponsored by that journal for the purpose of establishing the need to revise and update the *Humanist Manifesto* of 1933. Blanshard wrote as follows:

. . . We have an obligation to expose and attack the world of religious miracles, magic, Bible-worship, salvationism, heaven, hell, and all the mythical deities. We should be particularly specific and energetic in attacking such quack millennialists as Billy Graham and such embattled reactionaries as Pope Paul VI because they represent the two greatest anti-humanist aggregates in our society.

The Humanist, March–April, 1973

This statement by Paul Blanshard summarizes the true heart of the humanist position—its rejection of the Bible, Christ, and salvation.

THE NEW *MANIFESTO*

In September of 1973, the American Humanist Association, acting jointly with the American Ethical Union, released the final text of *Humanist Manifesto II*. This document proved to be far more than a mere revision of the 1933 *Manifesto*. The 1973 statement represents an entirely new effort to express the philosophy of humanism to a world still groaning under the burdens which *Manifesto I* had failed to alleviate in the past four decades.

The full text of *Humanist Manifesto II* should be studied carefully by any reader who wishes to gain objective insight into the nature, purpose, and direction of the contemporary humanist movement. The document is upwards of four thousand words in length. It consists of a preface, an introduction and seventeen points organized under six major headings: Religion, Ethics, The Individual, Democratic Society, World Community, and Humanity as a Whole. The names of 114 signers, among whom are nine Unitarian ministers, two rabbis, and two professors of religion, are appended to the statement.

The preface states that "It is forty years since *Humanist Manifesto I* (1933) appeared." Events since then make that earlier statement seem "far too optimistic." The past forty years have witnessed Nazism, inhuman wars, police states, unyielding racism, poverty, and other evils. An "affirmative and hopeful vision" is needed as we approach the twenty-first century. *Humanist Manifesto II* is said to be "a positive declaration for times of uncertainty."

ASSAULT ON CHRISTIANITY

Immediately, in the very next paragraph of the preface, a scathing attack on Christianity is launched. The idea of a "prayer-hearing God" is said to be "an unproved and outmoded faith." "Salvationism, based on mere affirmation, still appears as harmful, diverting people with false hopes of heaven hereafter. Reasonable minds look to other means for survival." It should be noted with care that this initial anti-God statement appears in the third paragraph of the preface, immediately following the claim that *Manifesto II* is "a positive declaration."

The introduction boldly proclaims that "the next century can be and should be the humanistic century." Traditional moral codes are no longer adequate. Belief is needed in the possibilities of human progress. The "set of common principles" contained in this manifesto represents "a design for a secular society on a planetary scale." This new *Humanist Manifesto* is presented "for the future of mankind" as "a vision of hope."

SELF-SALVATION AND "RIGHTS"

Understandably, *Religion* is the first of the six major topics discussed. ". . . traditional dogmatic or authoritarian religions that place revelation, God, ritual, or creed above human needs and experience do a disservice to the human species." The authors flatly declare, ". . . we find insufficient evidence for belief in the existence of a supernatural; it is either meaningless or irrelevant to the question of the survival and fulfillment of the human race. As nontheists, we begin with humans not God, nature not deity . . . ."

The humanist program to rule God out of the affairs of men is brought into sharp focus in the final sentence of the very first section with the statement, "No deity will save us: we must save ourselves." The second section states that promises of "immortal salvation or fear of eternal damnation" are both "illusory and harmful." Man has emerged from "natural evolutionary forces," and there is "no credible evidence that life survives the death of the body."

The third and fourth sections of the *Manifesto* fall under the general heading of *Ethics.* According to Point Three, ". . . moral values derive their source from human experience. Ethics is *autonomous* and *situational*, needing no theological or ideological sanction." The fourth section calls for the application of "reason and intelligence" and "the controlled use of scientific method" for the solution of human problems.

The fifth and sixth sections relate to the individual. ". . . We reject all religious, ideological, or moral codes that denigrate the individual, suppress freedom, dull intellect, dehumanize personality." Section 6 decries "intolerant attitudes" toward sexuality, which are often cultivated by "orthodox religions and puritanical cultures." The right to "birth control, abortion, and divorce should be recognized."

NATIONAL AND WORLD PROBLEMS

Sections 7 through 11 deal with democratic society, calling for "a full range of civil liberties," the right to die with dignity, euthanasia, and the right to suicide. The commitment to "an open and democratic society" is voiced, and the statement is made that "bureaucratic structures" should be held to a minimum. The separation of church and state is imperative. Economic systems should be evaluated on the basis of their ability to "increase the sum of human satisfaction, and enhance the quality of life." The "principle of moral equality" should be upheld in matters of race, religion, sex, age, and national origin. There should be adequate care for the unfortunate, and universal education should be provided for all.

Sections 12 through 17 are presented under the general heading *World Community*. Nationalism is to be deplored. A world community needs to be built, commensurate with the development of "a system of world law and world order based upon transnational federal government." Violence and force must be renounced as a method of solving international disputes. War is obsolete. International courts must be established for peaceful adjudication of differences. The resources of the earth must be conserved, and it is the obligation of the more developed nations to provide "massive technical, agricultural, medical, and economic assistance" to the less-developed portions of the world. "World poverty must cease." Communication and transportation across frontiers must be expanded, and travel restrictions must no longer be imposed.

Under a closing section entitled *Humanity as a Whole,* a ringing appeal is made for "commitment to all humankind" as "the highest commitment of which we are capable." We must move toward "a wider vision of human potentiality," with each person becoming "a citizen of a world community."

The unyielding optimism of *Manifesto II* is evident in its very last sentence: "We believe that humankind has the potential intelligence, good will, and cooperative skill to implement this commitment in the decades ahead."

MAN IN REBELLION

Christians will recognize *Humanist Manifesto II* as a pathetic document created by lost men tottering on the brink of eternity and whistling into the darkness of space. It is a document in which man has ruled his Creator out of existence. It asserts that man is good and God is bad. Accordingly, man has no source of values, no ultimate point of reference, no high commitment, no hope except in himself. Man finds his reason for being in the mere fact of his existence rather than in the service of the God of the universe. Man expresses his contempt for ultimate reality, for eternity, for life beyond the doorway of death. Humanism is man's effort to eliminate God from his thinking and to live as if God did not exist. It is man attempting to solve his problems apart from God. It is man in league with Satan and in rebellion against the authority of the Most High. It is man's effort to construct his own heaven on earth, without the help of our Lord and Savior, Jesus Christ.

A few appropriate words from God, selected from chapter 38 of Job, are appropriate for all humanists:

"Where were you when I laid the foundation of the earth! Have you ever in your life commanded the morning, And caused the dawn to know its place; Have you entered into the springs of the sea? Or have you walked in the recesses of the deep? Who has cleft a channel for the flood, Or a way for the thunderbolt; Can you bind the chains of the Pleiades, Or loose the cords of Orion? Do you know the ordinances of the heavens, Or fix their rule over the earth?"

CHRISTIANS AND HUMANISM

It is highly important for Christians everywhere to recognize the nature and intent of the rising humanist movement. More and more it is necessary for the discerning Christian to apply the following acid test to all ideologies and to the policies and platforms of new groups which appear on the scene: "Is it of God, or is it of man?" The same test should be applied when humanism manifests itself in the educational system, in the world of politics, in economics, literature, art, entertainment, foreign policy, business, philosophy, religion, and elsewhere.

The only adequate answer to humanism is true Christianity, expressed consistently in all areas of life. Bible study *is* important—but it isn't enough. Attending church *is* important—but it isn't enough. Personal soul-winning is also very important—but it isn't sufficient to stem the tide of Godless humanism, which has already taken control of our schools, our courts, our economy, our government, and many of our churches. If Christianity-as-usual could turn back the oncoming tide of humanist influence, it would already have done so.

What is needed in this hour is a living dynamic faith in

Jesus Christ and His Resurrection power—a faith which will produce a great new emphasis on Christianity-in-action. Christians must become very practical. We must study the Bible with a purpose. We must study the Bible to discover the great principles which provide guidance and direction for the people of God today. We must formulate programs based on the Word of God and move into action with these programs—in education, business, law enforcement, morals, communications, public leadership, and government.

The moving force behind humanism is Satan. Humanism is basically Satan's philosophy and program. Certain features of it may sound reasonable, but it always leads to tragedy, simply because it ignores the guidance of God. Only our Christian citizens have the discernment to evaluate humanism for what it is. Therefore our Christian citizens represent the only force capable of defeating it.

CONFRONTATION AND CONSTRUCTIVENESS

However, we Christians must be realistic. We must realize that we cannot simply "wish" the devil's age-long program away. We must do battle openly against it. We must engage in an open confrontation with evil in all areas of life. Christians everywhere must believe the Word of God and follow up with the action which that belief produces. Do you doubt that this is practical?

> What use is it, my brethren, if a man says he has faith, but he has no works? Can that faith save him? If a brother or sister is without clothing and in need of daily food, and one of you says to them, "Go in peace, be warmed and be filled," and yet you do not give them what is necessary for their body, what use is that? Even so faith, if it has no works, is dead, being by itself.
>
> James 2:14–17

What is your faith producing these days? Are you trusting
God to enable you to change things you do not like? Is it
happening? You see, your faith is dead and useless if it ac-
complishes nothing. Christianity must be practical and effec-
tual against the mounting turbulence of our age or it is
worthless. We must look to God for energy to set forth on a
campaign of advancing the truth of God's Word both locally
and nationally.

Christians of all denominations must openly fight for
righteousness whenever and wherever humanism in any form
raises its evil head. We must develop constructive, biblically
based programs designed to deal effectively with the whole
range of problems and issues which afflict us today. These
programs must be rooted in eternal truth so as to assure their
effectiveness. And they must reflect glory and praise to
Almighty God, the Creator of all things.

> Put on the full armor of God, that you may be able to
> stand firm against the schemes of the devil. For our struggle
> is not against flesh and blood, but against the rulers, against
> the powers, against the world forces of this darkness, against
> the spiritual forces of wickedness in the heavenly places.
> Therefore, take up the full armor of God, that you may be
> able to resist in the evil day, and having done everything,
> to stand firm.
>
> Ephesians 6:11–13

In this chapter we have attempted to distinguish sharply
between the two basic approaches to the solution of problems
in the life of man on earth. Probably most people of faith
will grasp the distinction quite readily. But still much confusion persists among sincere Christians. This confusion is
especially evident whenever members of the family of God

begin to think about their role and responsibility in relation to the world of problem-ridden men in which they live for the present time. Next, an attempt will be made to clear up a measure of the confusion which exists in relation to a number of important topics which are frequently discussed by Christians.

4

Seven Areas of Confusion

Confusion reigns where purpose is lacking. Confusion disappears when we take the trouble to dig deeper for the truth.

Christians can be confused people. They shouldn't be, but too frequently they are. Unfortunately, knowledge of the Scriptures doesn't always dispel the differences which divide and separate Believers. Seven major topics on which confusion reigns especially are the Social Gospel, Christian Pietism, Theocracy, Utopianism, the role of the Christian in the Local Community, National Issues, and the End-Time.

THE SOCIAL GOSPEL

The sometimes-called *social-gospel* approach to problem solving was stated by John Lindsay of New York in response to a question directed to him by Tracy Early (*The Christian Century*, March 31, 1971).

"Is it appropriate," asked Mr. Early, "for churches to become specific in their political involvement to the extent of endorsing a particular piece of legislation, such as the proposal for welfare reform?"

Mr. Lindsay's reply was unequivocal: "Absolutely. They should be totally engaged in an effort to bring about changes in the system. They should be pursuing specific legislation, lobbying for it, talking about it publicly, using the pulpit as a forum for debate on the question, explaining its relation to questions of morality. I'm for all that."

This is a fairly typical statement of the social-gospel viewpoint. Social improvement through political action quite apart from Christian evangelism is the basic idea. A considerable number of denominational leaders, church agency officials, clergymen, and laymen are committed to this approach, although it is not as popular as it once was. Those who adhere to this view belong, almost exclusively, to the ranks of Modern Protestant Liberalism, which does not emphasize the biblical basis of Christian faith and action. Adherents of this view are motivated by a certain humanistic optimism which sees the solution of social problems as best achieved through schemes designed to manipulate the external environment. The proclamation of the Gospel of the crucified and risen Christ is not essential to the approach.

Carl F. H. Henry has focused attention on the major defects of the Social Gospel concept:

> . . . The Social Gospel . . . abandoned a Biblical-theistic view of man and the world for a speculative-pantheistic view . . . . While the idealistic or pantheistic rationale of liberal theology has collapsed, the Social Gospel movement survives mainly as a political thrust. Its distinguishing feature is the confidence that alteration of social structures quite independently of evangelism can insure a new world . . . . The Social Gospel became readily identified with a Socialist and sometimes Communist critique of

society, with espousal of a welfare state based on the political redistribution of wealth.

A Plea for Evangelical Demonstration

It is my position that Christian citizens should be concerned with the entire range of social, economic, and political problems, and that the church should encourage them to be active in these areas. Groups of church members should be formed for the explicit purpose of relating Christianity to the social scene at the local, state, and national levels. Such activity must be solidly based on a dynamic faith in the Christ of redemption, if it is to be worthy of Him or effective in the long run. Persistent evangelistic activity and biblical instruction which reaches the inner life and re-creates the individual spiritually is the only sure foundation on which worthwhile and enduring changes in the external realities of the life of man may be brought about.

A second criterion of success, as well as of Christian propriety, is that political action should seldom be undertaken *in the name of the church itself.* It should rather be undertaken by members and friends of the church acting as private citizens or organized groups. Active "political involvement" is not the mission of churches or denominations. It is, however, the necessary and continuing responsibility of the people of God as citizens in a free society.

CHRISTIAN PIETISM

Philip Jakob Spener, who began in 1670 to popularize pietism within the German Lutheran Church, was concerned about the intellectual dogmatism which had captivated the Christian community. In his devotional meetings he stressed Bible study, fellowship, and the participation of laymen in the spiritual ministry of the church. Worldly entertainments such as theatrical performances, dancing, and rowdy public games were denounced. To Spener and his followers, Christianity was essentially personal—an experience of the heart. The pietistic movement led by Spener and his successor, August Hermann Francke, was much needed in seventeenth- and eighteenth-century Europe. Its emphasis on the devotional dimensions of life made it a constructive, balancing influence. This emphasis has spread out to bless the entire Christian world in the past three centuries, and it is much in evidence today. Historically, pietism has even produced many worthy examples of Christian social application.

But among Evangelical Christians in the twentieth century the pietistic pendulum has all too frequently swung to such an extreme that it has, in the words of David O. Moberg, ". . . led many selfishly to try to escape from the world and live lazily in separation from it while waiting for Christ's coming instead of working in it until His return . . ." (*The Great Reversal*).

Beautiful as it is to enjoy the spiritual luxuries of a close walk with God each moment of every day, this orientation too frequently "degenerates into a smug and nagging moralism" (Will Herberg, *Protestant-Catholic, Jew*). The "Christian dropout" of today cannot discharge Christian responsibility by means of monkish withdrawal from reality, sugarcoated with "spiritual" clichés. Spirit-motivated living and action will relate to the worlds of business, economics, government, education, sports, medicine, law, and to all other categories of human experience.

THEOCRACY

"Rule over us!" shouted the men of Israel to Gideon after he had delivered the nation from the Midianite scourge.

Declining the invitation, Gideon replied: "I will not rule over you, nor shall my son rule over you; the Lord shall rule over you" (Judges 8:23).

Writing on the subject of *Theocracy* in the *International Standard Bible Encyclopedia,* W. M. McPheeters credits the Jewish soldier-historian Flavius Josephus (A.D. 37–95) with having coined the designation of this form of government in the following passage:

> Our lawgiver had an eye to none of these [commonly known forms of government] . . . but, as one might say, using a strained expression, he set forth the national polity as a theocracy, referring the rule and might to God . . . .

The word *theocracy* is composed of the two Greek nouns *theós* (God) and *krátos* (power). Although the term is not found in the Bible, the concept of theocracy is exclusively biblical in origin. In fact, this sharply defined idea of the rule of God over men is not found in any other literature, ancient or modern. The Old Testament notion of theocracy was that no agency of government could exercise independent power. The sure will of God, as declared by priests and prophets, or as reduced to writing in the form of a code of laws, was the sole standard of decision. As Gideon put it, "The Lord shall rule over you."

Prior to the reign of Saul, the government of Israel did approach the theocratic standard at certain times. However, it became evident that priests and prophets could defect— and the written law of God could be perverted. Therefore the practice of theocracy broke down, and the prophets of Israel and Judah recorded their visions of a glorious future day when the theocratic ideal will be restored—when the Divine Messiah-King will rule in righteousness. Theocracy in its pure form will feature His direct rule over all mankind. This will be the best possible form of government ever to exist.

Only God can establish a theocracy. Human attempts at establishment of societies based on utopian theocratic ideals have generally resulted in widespread injustice, oppression and even inquisition. Augustine's *City of God* (about A.D. 415) provided the basis of much visionary theocratic thought throughout the Middle Ages—but misery and squalor persisted on a mass scale. The realization of true theocracy must await the sovereign intervention of the Divine Person Himself in history.

Christian citizens should make no attempt to "bring in the Kingdom" by means of human effort. This is manifestly impossible. On the other hand, we Christians must not suspend the practice of biblical principles throughout the entire spectrum of life today simply because the Lord from heaven will one day return and assume His rightful headship of world government.

While the return of Christ represents the fulfillment of the divine plan of the ages and of all Christian hope, no man knows the divine schedule precisely. Those who will apply their Christian faith today must be obedient to the numerous scriptural exhortations to *occupy*, to *work* and to *walk* as members of the body of Christ in a world which will not now admit Christ as the Sovereign Head of all its affairs.

UTOPIANISM

From ancient times, men of imagination have shared their dreams of bright and happy societies devoid of poverty, misery, and the exploitation of man by man. Through neatly conceived phases of dialectical discourse Plato constructed

The Republic. Augustine in the fifth century portrayed a sort of theocratic utopia based on the implementation of divinely revealed principles.

Sir Thomas More's concept as sketched in his *Utopia* (1516) introduced the word itself into Western vocabularies. More's picture of the ideal state where all is ordered for the best interests of mankind as a whole is in the tradition of Plato's *Republic. The City of the Sun* (1623) by Tommaso Campanella, *The New Atlantis* (1627) by Francis Bacon, and *Commonwealth of Oceana* (1656) by James Harrington followed in the wake of this same politically oriented utopian tradition.

These conceptions were characterized by confidence in the natural order and faith in the basic goodness of man. With the development of modern science and the advent of technology, the modern era of utopian thought was born. Francis Bacon gave birth to this trend in *The New Atlantis* with its description of a society governed by scientists—a society which, as Bacon envisioned it, could and should come to exist in reality.

Beginning about the middle of the nineteenth century, Karl Marx and Friedrich Engels laid the foundations of modern socialist political-economic theory. They and their followers proclaimed the inevitable coming of the ideal state by means of political revolution and economic collectivism. In tragic contrast to the ancient utopians—whose thought was permeated with the pessimistic mood of stoicism, and who regarded any demand for a perfect society as a game to be played only by madmen—the Marxist utopians arose with violent fury to implement their dreams in society.

The end of their atheistic unrealism has been witnessed in the Soviet Union, in Mainland China, in Cuba, Chile, Rumania, Poland, and Yugoslavia. In these and in other socialist states economic want and social chaos, held in check only by police-state power, have merged in full view. Utopia was envisioned and attempted, but anti-utopia was produced. Aldous Huxley's *Brave New World* and George Orwell's *1984* portray, in stark reality, the true character of the resultant societies.

Utopian dreaming might well be a psychologically relaxing and constructive pursuit of those who wish to indulge in fantasy. No apparent harm can follow from the influence of poets, philosophers, and novelists who provide this form of escapism. An occasional flight to some lost horizon is good medicine for the prisoner of modern technological society with all of its rigors and stresses. The real danger comes when men attempt to implement, by means of the riot, the firebomb, and the gun, the shadowy musings of their unregenerate imaginations.

Those who are serious about the application of Christianity in society must be able to distinguish reality from unreality. They must be skilled in the art of separating fact from fantasy. They must bring to social problems the reserve, the balance, the stability with which only the Holy Spirit endows men. They must use their influence to check the extreme tendencies of unprincipled strong leaders who are bound to arise from time to time—leaders intent on turning their fantasies into reality through coercive means.

Drawing his perspective on social issues from the Word of God and keen observation of the current scene, the Christian citizen should involve himself as actively as possible in well-planned efforts—frequently nonpolitical in approach —designed to exert an influence for righteousness, morality, and decency within the community of men.

Christians must resist the alluring temptation of utopian idealism. Utopian schemes are impossible of implementation due to biblically assured defects in human nature. If "all men were angels," some of the utopian schemes might well be within the range of possibility. But the Word of God declares unequivocally that man's original defection from the will of God resulted in a basic depravity of nature which extended to the entire race. Such depravity has been in evidence throughout history—in the modern era as much as in former times. It persists as the most basic problem of man, his institutions, and his government.

Christian citizens of a free republic must operate within the framework of the given realities of human nature as well as cultural, social, economic, legal, and political considerations. They must strive to effect change whenever and wherever careful Christian evaluation leads to the conclusion that change is needed—and they must seek to do so by Christian means and in a Christian manner.

THE LOCAL COMMUNITY

"All of this social bunk is not my business," said a prominent evangelical minister when asked what his congregation was doing about a certain moral problem in his community. "My calling is to preach the Word of God, to win lost souls to Christ, and to teach my people how to live the Christian life. When I do this faithfully, I feel that I am doing all I can to influence the community for the good. The way to change the community is to win more people to Christ. If we win enough people to Christ, the nude bar and the pornographic theater will go out of business."

The minister was, in fact, a citizen of the community as well as a preacher. But through a rather typical process of pious Christian rationalization, he had talked himself out of assuming his rightful role in the local community. He refused to participate in any form of direct challenge to the merchandising of public evils right in the immediate area in which he and his church members, friends, and neighbors were rearing their children.

The minister's failure to exert leadership in direct opposition to evil forces in his community provided members of his congregation with the best possible excuse for doing nothing. They did, in fact, emulate the lethargy of their spiritual leader. They fully believed that their sole task was to "win people to Christ," and not to soil their garments in any potential conflict with corrupt business interests or the city administration.

Meanwhile, a majority of the members of the local city council were deeply concerned about the intrusion of pornographic interests into the community for the first time. They were concerned, and they wanted to do something about it. But they lacked one essential ingredient without which no program would stand even a chance of succeeding against such salacious interests—powerful and well funded as they were. That essential ingredient was *public support*.

The average Christian is secluded from the realities of community life. He has no idea how necessary public support is to those civic leaders who desire to maintain reasonable standards of decency in the local environment. Frequently such leaders are in no position to request openly the support of citizens. This can make them vulnerable to the charge that the viewpoint of those who stand with them is not representative of the community as a whole. This is an especially crucial factor in moral matters, since Supreme Court rulings have on several occasions in the past focused on the question of recognized community standards.

To be most effective, community support of the more highly motivated civic leaders should be spontaneous, widespread, and decisive. The businessmen, professional people, workers, housewives, and young citizens who comprise the membership of the evangelical churches of the community represent the most powerful resource of all for the support of righteous causes and opposition to unrighteous ones. If dedicated Christians fail to provide such initiative, who will?

In the second chapter of his letter to the Philippian Christians, the Apostle Paul exhorted them to regard others as more important than themselves. "Do not merely look out for your own personal interests, but also for the interests of others," wrote the apostle (Philippians 2:4). Undoubtedly there are dozens of ways in which an exhortation of this kind can be implemented. Certainly one way is to be sufficiently interested in the moral well-being of the sons and daughters of fellow Christians, friends and neighbors, to lend a righteous hand in an effort to keep pornography, gambling, drug addiction, alcoholism, and prostitution out of the very environment in which they are rearing their children.

Christians today need to be reprogrammed for a total approach to life in all of its dimensions. The minister is correct in pointing out that his primary task is evangelism and the edification of the saints. He is incorrect in believing that his responsibility and that of the members of his congregation does not extend beyond the sanctified portals of personal piety. Constructive action should always follow saving faith. If it doesn't, the genuineness of the faith itself is in question.

In addition to being members of Christ's body, the clergyman and those who gather to his ministry are also members of their local community. Whether they act or fail to act, their influence is felt in the community, directly or indirectly. This is an incontrovertible fact arising from the very nature of the electoral process and civic organization in all free societies. Christians, of all people, should be more discerning, more concerned, and more active in support of righteousness in the local community than any other category of citizens, including the members of political parties.

No minister should allow his theological training, his personal conditioning by his friends, or the traditions of his church as enunciated by the church board, to deny him the exercise of his full rights and responsibilities as an individual citizen of his community. Outside his church he should be free to speak out publicly, even on the most controversial of issues, so long as he makes it clear that he does so as a private citizen, and not as a spokesman for his congregation.

The minister who manifests a personal concern for the community, and who conducts himself appropriately, will be rewarded with the deep appreciation and good will of the finest elements of the community, both within and without his church. Whatever hostility his righteous influence may arouse from opposing forces should be sustained with patience and Christian grace.

NATIONAL ISSUES

Just as a Christian should assume a constructive role in his local community, he should likewise be aware of major issues confronting the nation. The Christian citizen should apply his powers of discernment in sifting out the most crucial issues for top-priority attention. He should make it his business to gather information, to search his Bible for divine perspective on the pertinent issues, to formulate a plan of Christian action, to enlist the aid of fellow citizens, and to launch and develop the most effective possible program designed to influence the public for the good in relation to those particular issues.

Christian application relative to national issues involves establishment of power bases, planned efforts, and organized groups. Cool-headed Christian strategy formulation, followed up with effective group action, can turn the tide of public opinion, overwhelm legislators and other officials, and win the day for righteousness in the continuing war between the forces of light and darkness.

THE END-TIME

A friend, convinced that the Lord is going to return almost immediately, asked, "Why bother with society and its problems? Why bother with economics? Why bother with ecology or any of these other problems? Why bother with anything but the Gospel? Man has made a mess of things and this world is going down. Why polish brass on a sinking ship?"

Well, there are good reasons why a Christian should "polish brass," if by this is meant consistent Christian living and application. First, we don't know when the Lord is going to return. It might be soon—but then again it might be another thousand years. The "signs of the times" are increasingly evident, but we simply do not know God's schedule. Martin Luther thought he was living in the end time in the sixteenth century. Certain cultists have wrapped themselves in white sheets and gone to the hilltops in readiness to be snatched away. The fact of the matter is that none of us knows God's schedule. The New Testament admonishes us to be ready, while at the same time "running the race" of the Christian life.

Christians who love their children ought to be concerned about Christian application. To the degree that we are influential in bringing about the improvement of the total spiritual-ideological-material environment in which our children are being reared, we express our love for them. Normal love for our offspring should prompt us to bend every effort to assure that our children will not in the future be engulfed in some new form of totalitarianism, for example.

Withdrawal from the world with all of its challenges and problems is not the answer. Mature Christians will recognize the absurdity of that form of neomonasticism which afflicts many of our fine Christian friends today. Withdrawal of that kind has no foundation in the Bible, in history, or in a realistic assessment of the time and cultural context in which we live in this modern world. Such withdrawal can only be interpreted as refusal to fulfill the Creation mandate of Genesis 1:28—the divine commission to subdue the earth and rule over created things.

Those who have made consistent application of Christian truth in the past have influenced the direction of history. The New Testament nowhere suggests that Christians should suspend the practice of righteousness because Christ's return is imminent. We live in a time in which those Christian values which underlie civilization are being gravely challenged from numerous sources. Our task, as Christians, is to proclaim the Gospel of our crucified and risen Savior, and to follow up with dynamic Christian application in all areas of life, with confidence in God and joy in the realization that ultimately all things are in His hands.

CONCLUSION

The movement to apply Christianity in our nation will succeed because it is rooted in basic reality—the truth of God.

In a certain sense there are only two classes of people—those who live by truth and those who do not. Moses was guided by truth; Pharaoh was not. Paul perceived reality;

Emperor Nero did not. Christian principles can be applied properly to the problems of men only by those who are guided by the immutable truth of God.

A movement rooted in truth will prevail; a movement rooted in humanistic calculations will fail in time.

The success of a movement is determined not by the elevation of its instigators to power, but by its elevation of truth and reality to prominence.

A movement motivated by transitory principles is unworthy of sacrifice. A movement motivated by eternal principles will command supreme sacrifice.

A movement which elevates eternal principles is a success, even if its champions all go down to martyrdom. A movement which tramples eternal principles is a failure, even if its leaders are elevated to the helm of state.

Sincere believers in Jesus Christ everywhere should thank God for the emerging movement of Christian citizens who intend to be victorious because Almighty God, the sovereign source of all truth and reality, is on the throne of this universe, guiding and empowering them.

For the most part, biblical principles are not being applied widely to the problems confronting our community and nation. Belief in the Bible does not necessarily result in effective action. The great majority of Christians are interested only in the personal dimensions of Christianity. Theirs is an egocentric faith; the big *me* is prominent. Their faith begins with Christ and ends with self. The tragedy of our time is the failure of so many sincere Christians to apply the truths and principles of the Bible faithfully and consistently throughout the whole spectrum of social-political reality.

Large numbers of Evangelical Christians in America are amazingly lethargic. They listen with great excitement to thrilling sermons and Bible studies, but they are almost totally lacking in discernment relative to the larger issues of today. They are doing little or nothing about Christian application in the broader sense.

Needed today is a vast new movement to activate Christians and get them involved in the application of their faith. A spirit-filled life should be an action-filled life. Christian truth must be applied in all areas of life, thought, and activity. That is the primary meaning of *Applied Christianity.*

It is great to have a Savior who is adequate for the individual, but God never intended for that individual Christian to turn all of his blessings inward for his own selfish satisfaction exclusively. Genuine Christianity ought to flow outward. Christian responsibility extends to the family, the business, the academy, the community, the nation, and to the ideologies which shape our culture and give direction to civilization.

Too frequently in the past, the most sincere Christians have allowed the events of their time to pass them by. Hardly discerning the significance of these events and lacking the motivation to act in Christian conscience, they have been engulfed in unspeakable horrors. In the next section we will see that God has prepared a special people to live as lights in a dark world—a people who alone possess the vision, the discernment, the sense of responsibility, the moral character, and the heaven-wrought inspiration needed to deal constructively and effectively with the multitudinous ills which beset our society and threaten our civilization.

PART II

The People

If men, not merely nominally Christians, but of real religion and sincere piety, joined with abilities, were advanced and called up to office in every civil department, how would it countenance and recommend virtue! But, alas! is there not too much Laodiceanism in this land? Is not Jesus in danger of being wounded in the house of his friends?

VERNA M. HALL, compiler, *Christian History of the Constitution*

Ours is a world beset with problems. Special insight is required if keen, realistic analysis is to be made. Unwavering stability is needed, if an enlightened viewpoint is to be upheld. High courage is required to render decisions and to follow through with vital action rooted in principle rather than expediency, even in the face of great odds. God has prepared a unique people who possess, potentially, those spiritual and moral virtues which qualify them for the leadership needed to bolster the structures and institutions of civilization.

5

Christian Statesmen of the Past

Christianity pervades human culture, influencing the thought systems of great people who might not even belong to the ranks of the "born again." Men like Jefferson and Franklin were not Christians in the evangelical sense, but in a wider meaning they were children of Christianized civilization— and they in turn contributed to it. God sent them to us.

Many examples of Christian statesmanship come to us from out of the long past. Christians in key positions have fought for causes which have unshackled slaves, preserved peace, abolished unjust laws, lifted tyranny, raised the standard of living, restrained the predatory nature of man, elevated human dignity, and banished superstition. Let's look at some of the historical figures who have exemplified Christian principles in the arena of public leadership.

WILLIAM WILBERFORCE

In the year 1800, Great Britain led the world in slave trade. British ships plied the seas between Africa and the

New World. Their main cargo was black human beings, chained in pairs on crude shelves with only two and a half feet of head room. By the time they reached America or the West Indies, usually 10 percent would be dead. Others would be desperately ill. On certain occasions, when a ship would flounder in a storm, the wretched slaves would be dumped overboard without compunction or mercy. Male slaves who made it to the new land would bring as much as forty pounds per head. For England, the slave trade was legalized national policy, inseparably linked with commerce and the national security.

Some of the Christians, like John Wesley and a few of the Quakers, had the courage to speak up and denounce this evil practice. But their voices were powerless to bring change. It was one thing to rise in protest in the public square, and quite another to carry the fight into Parliament, where any policy change would have to be effected. This required a man strong enough to turn the whole tide of English commercial and political interest, bold enough to attempt the impossible, and persistent enough to persevere in the face of the most crushing hostility and bitterness of evil men.

Such a giant was a Christian named William Wilberforce, and it was he who spearheaded the movement which brought about the abolition, first of slave trade, and later of slavery itself. All of this happened in his own lifetime.

Elected to Parliament in 1780, Wilberforce took up the struggle to abolish slavery inside the halls of his country's top legislative body. Year after year he persisted, bringing the matter up for discussion, presenting the case against the slave trade with all the force of his character, first gaining a small following and then enlarging it—until one February night when Parliament voted to abolish the slave trade. At that moment a colleague and partner arose and hailed Wilberforce as the savior of countless lives, and every man in the House sprang to his feet to join in the thunderous harmony of applause—while the humble Wilberforce sat in his seat and wept.

Who was this giant? A humble, spiritual Christian. A man who communed with God day by day, drawing his nourishment from the spiritual milk of the Word. Where are the young men of this generation who will enter into the halls of Congress dedicated to combat evil and to fight for righteousness?

A small army of young men and women marches out of our pagan secular universities every year, carrying diplomas. Many of these are moral delinquents. Some find their way into public life to place their hands on the rudder of the ship of state. But equally brilliant Christian students, engaging in pious nonsense, smugly convince themselves that, because their citizenship is in heaven, they have no responsibility to take a hand in so mundane a task as manning the helm.

WILLIAM E. GLADSTONE

Another great Christian statesman was William E. Gladstone, whose noble life spanned almost the entire nineteenth century. Four times Prime Minister of England, he brought to the helm of Great Britain enlightened Christian leadership in a day in which powerful interests held tenaciously to the arrogant colonial policies of the past. Towering above his generation, he brought his Christian perspective to bear on matters of empire, refusing to descend to the low level of petty political prejudice.

Gladstone was a financial genius, whose budgets showed

great fairness in distribution of the tax burdens. He instituted reforms in civil service, electoral procedures, court organization, and in many other fields. According to the *Columbia Encyclopedia,* his two Parliamentary reform acts of 1884 and 1885 "practically gave manhood suffrage to England."

Christian conscience with regard to social issues can be no stronger or better than the doctrine from which it arises. If that doctrine is sound, the outflow in terms of action should be pertinent. The firmness of Gladstone's doctrinal foundation is reflected in the title of his compilation of theological works—*The Impregnable Rock of Holy Scripture.*

LORD SHAFTESBURY

Perhaps the greatest Christian character of mid-nineteenth century England was Lord Shaftesbury (Anthony Ashley Cooper). He was a thoroughgoing Christian, who referred to himself as "an evangelical of the evangelicals." His biographer, G. F. A. Best, said of Shaftesbury:

> His was an activist as well as a meditative faith. All his concerns were religious, and all involved him in those social and political affairs, which he believed ought to reflect, at the institutional level, the religious interests of mankind. He rose from prayer or Bible study ready and eager to serve the Lord equally by local charity or imperial politics, and never felt any quality of difference between them.

It was characteristic of Shaftesbury to speak up on public issues whenever the behavior of his country came into conflict with his Christian conscience. When it was proposed that Queen Victoria assume the new title of *Empress,* he boldly led the opposition, reminding the Throne of England that it was upheld by the sentiment of the people and not by force or superstition. He expressed tender feelings toward the persecuted Irish, to whom he referred as "that wronged and insulted people." He sympathized with the Scottish people in their resistance to English aggression. He voiced his strong opposition to Austrian and Russian despotism.

Shaftesbury saw the role of Britain in Europe as one of moral influence and example. He was deeply hurt when the calamities of the Crimean War reflected on the lack of moral character of his country. He was openly sympathetic toward nationalist and constitutionalist movements. When France annexed Savoy, Shaftesbury thundered, "I protest against the policy of treating nations like flocks of sheep." His burning desire for righteousness and justice in the conduct of international affairs led him in 1843 to lodge a noble protest against British participation in the opium trade.

Shaftesbury was a man of faith. The moral and spiritual perspective which he gained through careful study of the Word of God was focused on the issues of his day. He favored policies which appeared to him to be consistent with the will of God as revealed in the Bible, and he opposed those which appeared otherwise.

ROGER WILLIAMS

A galaxy of Christian and Christian-influenced statesmen gathered around the colonial and revolutionary era of American history. Going back to the mid-seventeenth century, we find that the Puritans, who fled England to avoid religious persecution, had set up a tightly controlled religious tyranny in the Massachusetts colony. Like those who had mistreated them in the Old Country, they suppressed and persecuted people of other faiths.

In February of 1631, there came to Massachusetts from England a young man named Roger Williams. A Puritan himself, and thoroughly trained in theology, the young man was received with open arms. But within a short time, he had become the center of controversy. His offense was that he believed in freedom of conscience. When the Puritan leaders of Boston declared him a heretic, he boldly replied that the Boston Puritans themselves were heretical.

For his bold and uncompromising preaching of Christian freedom, Roger Williams was eventually driven from Massachusetts. He took to the wilderness and spent fourteen weeks among the trees, the animals, and the friendly Indians. During this time he planned a free colony, which he later established on land purchased from the Indians.

Roger Williams called his new colony *Providence.* In this unique sanctuary, Williams declared that every man would be the political equal of every other. He insisted on absolute separation of Church and State, individual dignity, and freedom of conscience.

Here was an entirely new concept—government by and for free men. It is significant that Rhode Island was the first of the original thirteen colonies to declare its independence from Great Britain. Williams's Doctrine of Christian Freedom had hacked out of the wilderness of the New World a place of refuge for the persecuted, and the whole American society was one day to become such a place.

WILLIAM PENN

Another Christian statesman of colonial times was William Penn. In her biography of Penn, Catherine Owens Peare described the Christian vision of the great Quaker. She said he envisioned "a world free of the debauchery of the times, the plagues of wars, a world unburdened by a nobility . . . ."

The great concern of William Penn for the welfare of earth-bound people is reflected in his description of the kind of city he wanted, when it came to establishing Philadelphia. Biographer Peare sketches it for us:

> . . . His city was not to grow up in an unplanned shamble, neither was it to suffer from the unwholesome crowding and congestion of London and Paris. Penn had seen London ridden by plague incubated within her own premises; he had seen her destroyed by fire and rebuilt largely upon the same unplanned, inconvenient lines . . . . He had in mind something quite different—an entire, planned city—a town with straight streets running "uniform down to the water from the country bounds," and "houses built upon a line," and every house placed in the "middle of its plat . . . so that there may be ground on each side for gardens and orchards, or fields, that it may be a green country town, which will never be burned, and always be wholesome."
>
> *William Penn,* p. 225

How many Christians today are concerned with the shapes of cities, or with the security, convenience and well-being of the people living in them?

William Penn was the architect of the original frame of government of Pennsylvania, the colony which he founded. In drafting this government out of his own experience, Christian perspective, and wisdom, Penn exhibited his true greatness. Even though he was undisputed master of the colony by legal charter from the British Crown, he renounced personal power in a way that was "extraordinary then and is still extraordinary in our times," wrote Catherine Peare. "It takes a great man to achieve power, a greater man to abrogate it, and in this moment of decision, when he resisted the temptations of personal power, William Penn rose to a level achieved by only a rare few."

With careful deliberation, and acting with his own hand, William Penn divested himself and his successors of any opportunity of subjecting the citizens of Pennsylvania to tyranny in any form. His enlightened political direction, drawn from the fountains of his Christian understanding, put the power in the people, laid a new foundation of liberty, and gave to the spirit of freedom a wider dimension than had ever been enjoyed under any definition of Anglo-Saxon organic law. It was consistent with Penn's principle "that no man or number of men upon earth hath power or authority to rule over men's consciences in religious matters."

Coming down to revolutionary times, American Christian statesmen are numerous. Almost all of our founding fathers were either committed Christians or men who were strongly under the influence of Christian moral philosophy.

SAMUEL ADAMS

Samuel Adams was a man of outspoken Christian conviction. He was Harvard-trained, a reader of theology, a man who at one time had planned a career in the ministry. Some have said that his influence was so great that the American Revolution might not even have occurred without him. Samuel Adams spoke of freedom as "the gift of God Almighty." He pointed the colonists to the New Testament for a better understanding of the principles of freedom. In his opposition to the inhuman policies of the English Crown, he declared, "I will oppose this tyranny at the threshold, though the fabric of liberty fall, and I perish in its ruin."

JOHN DICKINSON AND JOHN ADAMS

Writing in *Heroic Colonial Christians*, Henry W. Coray reminds us that John Dickinson, the Pennsylvanian who advised caution at the Convention which voted for independence, bowed his head and prayed audibly before beginning his great speech on that occasion. John Adams, who replied to the Dickinson speech, was the cousin of Samuel Adams and a Presbyterian elder. It was the historian George Bancroft who referred to the Revolution of 1776 as "a Presbyterian measure."

DR. JOHN WITHERSPOON

One great Presbyterian of the Revolution was Dr. John Witherspoon, president of the College of New Jersey (now Princeton University). He was a delegate to the Convention which adopted the Declaration of Independence, and the only clergyman to sign that document. When Woodrow Wilson became the president of Princeton 125 years later, he spoke in his inaugural address of "Princeton in the Nation's Service." It was John Witherspoon who first structured the college and its program with national service in view.

Certainly John Witherspoon was an outstanding figure of the Revolution. Equally adept as preacher, educator, politician, economist, lawmaker, and philosopher, he preached the Word of God in his pulpit, being careful to keep politics out of it. At the same time, in his role as a private citizen, he moved in the realm of government and stamped his Christian influence upon those chaotic times.

GEORGE WASHINGTON

When George Washington finally prevailed against the British forces, his gratitude to God was apparent. On April 18, 1783, he issued an order to suspend the fighting, including in the order the following words:

The Commander-in-Chief orders the cessation of hostili-
ties between the United States of America and the king of
Great Britain to be publicly proclaimed tomorrow at 12
o'clock . . . after which the chaplains with the several bri-
gades will render thanks to almighty God for all his mercies,
particularly for his overruling the wrath of man to his own
glory, and causing the rage of war to cease amongst the
nations.

> from *Basic Writings of George
> Washington,* edited by SAXE COMMINS

A few years after the Revolution, the victorious General
Washington returned to Princeton, where his armies had
once fought the Red Coats, as guest of honor of the university. In response to a welcoming speech honoring him,
Washington humbly promised that he would pray for the
blessing of heaven on the college, its head, its trustees, and
its faculty, that God would be pleased to prosper the institution and use it increasingly in promoting the cause of religion
and learning.

ABRAHAM LINCOLN

One of the great Christians who influenced American
history was the Great Emancipator, Abraham Lincoln. Like
Wilberforce, Lincoln saw human slavery as a violation of
human dignity, a moral outrage, and an offense against God.
More than any other human factor, it was the towering
Christian statesmanship of Abraham Lincoln that saw the
nation through that deluge of wrath. This was the man who
openly confessed his trust in the Almighty when he left
Springfield to assume the presidency in February, 1861.
This was the man who asked the people to uphold him in
prayer. This was the man who rebuked the people like a

prophet of old for ignoring the goodness of God in the life of the nation. This was the man who was magnanimous in victory, who appealed to those who were alienated and embittered by the terrors of war to "bind up the nation's wounds"—"with malice toward none, with charity for all."

CONCLUSION

Affirming the inseparable connection of Christianity with the foundation of our country, the great Daniel Webster declared:

> . . . let us not forget the religious character of our origin. Our fathers were brought hither by their veneration of the Christian religion. They journeyed by its light, and labored in its hope. They sought to incorporate its principles with the element of their society, and to diffuse its influence through all their institutions, civil, political, or literary. Let us cherish these sentiments, and extend this influence still more widely; in the full conviction, that this is the happiest society which partakes in the highest degree of the mild and peaceful spirit of Christianity.
>
> VERNA M. HALL, *Christian History of The Constitution*

Samuel Adams in *Rights of the Colonists* (1772) saw human freedom as derived from God.

> . . . The right to freedom being the gift of God Almighty . . . 'The Rights of the Colonists as Christians' . . . may be best understood by reading and carefully studying the institutes of the great Law Giver . . . which are to be found clearly written and promulgated in the New Testament.
>
> *Ibid*, p. XIII

In his famous letter to the clergymen of Philadelphia, March 3, 1797, George Washington gave his assessment of the relationship between Christianity and government:

> Believing, as I do, that *Religion* and *Morality* are the essential pillars of Civil society, I view, with unspeakable pleasure, that harmony and brotherly love, which characterizes the Clergy of different denominations, as well in this as in other parts of the United States; exhibiting to the world a new and interesting spectacle, at once the pride of our Country and the surest basis of Universal Harmony.
>
> NORMAN COUSINS, *In God We Trust*

The secular spirit of social idealism which is so widely heralded today has some worthy goals. But the program which the secular mind devises to give legs to its idealism is not rooted in Christian doctrine or faith in our Lord Jesus Christ. It is humanistic and socialistic rather than Christian. It ignores the theistic-spiritual dimension. It decries property rights, which the Bible upholds. It seeks to achieve its goals through initiative-deadening collectivism. It tries to solve human problems by means of the "something-for-nothing" myth of the welfare state. Through its so-called social-gospel concept, it perverts the spiritual role of the Church as the New Testament institution for evangelism. It redefines *democracy* to mean government management for the good of all, relegating individual freedom to the scrap heap of history.

The secular prescription for treating the social ills of our day has been tried and found wanting. An adequate corps of Christian leader-activists is needed to offer a reasonable alternative. If our country is to find its way out of the morass of its self-made wilderness at this point in history, Christians must guide the nation into the paths of righteousness.

How may Christians give directions to the ship of state?

In addition to their spiritual ministries, an effective way is to get aboard the ship, join the crew, and take a hand in sailing the vessel. A Christian representative or senator, judge, ambassador or president—a key person in a key position—may be the hinge on which the wisdom of God swings the affairs of men.

Let the Church adhere to its spiritual task of training, motivating, and inspiring our youth in the Christian way of life, so that they might be strong in the face of the challenges of our time. Thus prepared, let us encourage many of our brightest, most spiritual, and stable Christian young people to move out into the secular world of economics, law, government, education, and international affairs, as well as into the pulpit and the mission field. After all, the consistent practice of Christian faith in the secular world is as much a function of "the Christian way of life" as is Bible teaching and evangelism.

Next we will see that God has graciously given Christians special powers of discernment, which He expects them to exercise. Spiritual discernment is a primary qualification of leadership in a society suffering from numerous false philosophies.

6

Christian Discernment

Why have Christians so often been so blind to the meaning of the great events transpiring in our time? Is it because we haven't bothered to relate the Word of God to those affairs of life which lie beyond our personal interests, our families, and our immediate circle of Christian friends?

Deception is as old as Satan and the Garden of Eden. But its effectiveness as a tool for the manipulation of the minds of men has increased tremendously in our time. The technology of mass communications now makes it possible for one man to deceive masses of people—sometimes entire nations.

A tragic example is the deception which Adolph Hitler perpetrated on the German people at the time of his rise to power. Intellectuals, artists, businessmen, clergymen, students, housewives—people from all walks of life—were swept up in a gigantic national movement led by a madman gifted with extraordinary powers of speech.

DECEIVED CHRISTIANS

One of the most tragic aspects of the Hitler takeover was his success in deceiving the German Christians. As a Christian informant from Germany, who had lived through the holocaust of World War II, told me, "Most of the Bible-believing Christians of Germany were right on Hitler's bandwagon at the time of his rise to power. They felt that he made more sense than anyone else, that he was unifying the country, that he had a clear-cut plan in a time of deep confusion. These Christians were so busy with their Bible studies, their prayer meetings, their worship services, and their Christian fellowship that they were almost totally unaware of the controlling realities of the time."

Real Christian discernment was almost nonexistent, and there was little or no application of biblical truth to the whole spectrum of life. The very people who should have been the first to sound a loud warning concerning the sinister and foreboding developments in the German nation were asleep at the switch.

PAUL'S PRAYER BURDEN

Two thousand years ago the Apostle Paul was greatly concerned about Christian discernment. When he wrote his famous letter to the Philippian Christians, he summarized in a few words the content of his main prayer for them:

> And this I pray, that your love may abound still more and more in real knowledge and all discernment, so that you may approve the things that are excellent, in order to be sincere and blameless until the day of Christ; having been filled with the fruit of righteousness which comes through Jesus Christ, to the glory and praise of God.
>
> Philippians 1:9–11

The last word of verse nine is the key to our understanding of Paul's prayer burden for the Philippian Christians. The subject of this famous prayer, issued from a Roman prison dungeon, was *discernment*. In the original language, the word *aisthēsis* had reference to sense perception. Through usage, it came to mean quickness, alertness, readiness of mind, sensitivity to a situation, perception. Here in Philippians 1:9 it means *quickness to sense the true situation which exists—the ability to choose wisely between possible alternatives.*

In this prayer summarization, Paul discussed the *prerequisites* of discernment, the *practice* of discernment and the *product* or results of discernment, when it is practiced consistently in the Christian life.

PREREQUISITES OF DISCERNMENT

The two prerequisites, without which real discernment is impossible, are *love* and *knowledge*. The original word for *love* is the Greek word *agape*, which conveys the idea of divine, selfless, sacrificial love—the quality of love which moved our Lord Jesus Christ to the cross. We might translate it appropriately *superlove*. It is a prerequisite of Christian discernment. The more you love a person, the greater your discernment with regard to that person and his welfare. A mother is the most discerning person in all the world when it comes to the welfare of her child. The reason for this is that she loves the child in a very unique way.

The second prerequisite of discernment is *knowledge*. In the original language, the word that is translated *knowledge* (*epignōsis*) carries the meaning of full or complete knowledge—the kind of knowledge that comes from adequate learning of facts. A good illustration is the work of a skilled FBI investigator who delves into every fact relating to a case. He puts together all of the evidence available and runs it through the crime laboratory. Before he moves in and makes an arrest, he has achieved a very high degree of knowledge relative to the case he has been studying, and he has acquired an exceedingly high level of discernment. Equipped with "superknowledge," he makes his arrest and brings the criminal to justice. *Superlove* and *superknowledge* are the two prerequisites of *superperception* or Christian discernment.

DISTINGUISHING THINGS THAT DIFFER

Paul amplifies the meaning of Christian discernment in the first clause of verse ten. Discernment means the ability to "approve the things that are excellent," or, more literally, to "distinguish between the things that differ." This is the heart and core of Paul's prayer for the Philippians. God says things differ. Life is a sequence of decisions based on our choices between possible alternatives. God wants us to have superdiscernment in order to perceive the differences between these alternatives and to act accordingly.

The main work of Satan is deception. His deceptive activities are exposed by six different Hebrew words in the Old Testament and seven different Greek words in the New Testament, all of which are translated "deceive" in our English Bible. In Revelation 12:9, Satan is said to be the one who "deceives the whole world." So far as the Christian walk in this world is concerned, deception is the order of the day. God's gracious provision for this situation is Christian discernment—superdiscernment.

Amplifying the first clause of Philippians 1:10 to bring out the force of the original language, God wants us to be able to make fine distinctions between things which are different. What "things"? What does Paul mean when he refers to "the things which differ"? (*See* marginal note for

Philippians 1:10 NASV.) "Differences" exist everywhere.
There are different concepts, ideas, and approaches to every
subject, ideology, religion, philosophy, activity, or concern.
God wants the Christian to have a fine-tuned sense of superdiscernment. God wants the Christian to be able to recognize
the differences which exist with regard to any matter which
may confront him, so that he might throw his weight on the
side of righteousness.

SHRUGGING CHRISTIANS

Too frequently when we ask a Christian to state his position on a major issue of the day, he responds with a shrug.
We have all too many shrugging Christians these days. The
Christian shrug is a clear signal that the individual knows
little or nothing about the particular issue under discussion,
and that he probably cares less.

The shrugging Christian betrays the fact that he is in
danger of being deceived, tricked, trapped, taken, misled
into serving the cause of Satan rather than Christ. The cure
for this condition is superlove, wrought by the Holy Spirit,
and superknowledge, gained by self-discipline and thorough
study of facts. These capabilities will result in supersensi-
tive Christian discernment.

National opinion polls frequently list the top issues confronting our people. Issues like inflation, the energy shortage,
crime, drug abuse, race relations, communism, pollution, and
poverty appear to be of foremost concern today. Some additional issues which are screaming for attention revolve
around such subjects as education, labor, foreign policy,
capitalism, socialism, the role of technology, taxation, deficit
spending, corruption in public leadership, monetary and
fiscal policy, radicalism, humanism, women's liberation,

abortion, euthanasia, satanism, occult practices, business, and free enterprise.

The attitudes, decisions and activities of thousands of leaders and masses of people relative to crucial issues such as these will largely determine the direction of our culture. The response of modern men to these and other weighty issues will determine the shape of our society—the kind of civilization our kids will inherit tomorrow and tomorrow and tomorrow, until God shall draw the curtain on this present world order. Christians may withdraw and stand aloof from the decision-making process, or they may participate actively in it, utilizing the unique powers of discernment which the Lord has given them.

WHY SHOULDN'T CHRISTIANS PARTICIPATE?

Should millions of Christians limit their interests and activities to Bible studies, prayer meetings, and worship services? Should we fail to apply Christian truth in all areas of life? Why should we not actively discern the trends of the time, distinguish the things that differ, take a position that is in harmony with the Word of God and stand for it? Doesn't God want us to add virtue to our faith in all areas of life? In a day of convulsion and social upheaval, are Christians justified in playing the ostrich? Is mere passive participation in spiritual exercises pleasing to God?

Christian noninterest and nonaction can have a devastatingly negative effect on the image which we project to others. At a luncheon a bright young student from the University of New Mexico was overheard to complain, "There are a few Christians on my campus, but their Christianity is just a personal thing with them. It's all locked up inside of them. It relates to nothing that is happening in the world today!"

AN ACID TEST THAT WORKS

It might be objected that no individual Christian can possibly develop enough knowledge on every conceivable subject to exercise superdiscernment. The fact is, you need not know everything about a philosophical, ideological, social, economic, or political system in order to have effective Christian discernment. Simply turn the searchlight of Christian discernment on the presuppositions of the thought system. The acid test of any thought system is how it answers three short questions which relate to the three tenses of human experience:

1. What concept of origin does it teach? (Past)
2. What is its concept of the meaning and the purpose of life? (Present)
3. What is its concept of future events? (Future)

Let's see how this works. The French molecular biologist, Jacques Monod, has written a popular best-selling book entitled *Chance and Necessity*. In this book, Monod explains the origin of life in terms of "prebiotic chemical evolution" (page 140) and the formation, by chance, of "macromolecules capable, under the conditions prevailing in the primordial soup, of promoting their own replication unaided by any teleonomic apparatus" (page 141).

Monod doesn't prove his case on the origin of life; he just presupposes it! You don't need to be a molecular biologist in order to see that his idea clashes completely with the biblical creationist view of the origin of man. Therefore, the thought system put forward by Jacques Monod is revealed to be humanistic rather than Christian.

Professor B. F. Skinner has written a highly controversial

book entitled *Beyond Freedom and Dignity*. Much of the academic world is accepting its teachings. In this volume Skinner offers a viewpoint known as *behaviorism*. He teaches that a person's behavior is the result of conditioning by his environment. Man is nothing in himself. He is just a predetermined causal chain of happenings—a bundle of conditioning—a haphazard cluster of responses to environmental stimuli.

How does Skinner's thought system square with the Bible? It is antagonistic to the Word of God in its view of man, his origin, self-responsibility for his actions and destiny. A Christian may arrive at this conclusion quite easily as soon as he becomes aware of the substance of Skinner's position. It is not necessary to become a profound, lifelong scholar in order to get involved in effective Christian discernment, application, and action. It is actually quite easy to distinguish between the things that differ. Most of the satanic and humanistic thought systems differ radically from the Word of God. There is a clash of basic ideas. The differences are so glaring that you can't miss them.

We Christians must make it our business to acquaint ourselves with developments in the world of thought, to exercise Christian discernment, and to follow up with appropriate action.

WHAT KINDS OF ACTION?

Depending on the gifts and competence of the individual Christian, there are many action projects which may be undertaken. Assume, for example, that a Christian activist has just applied the Christian acid test to a book written by a Jacques Monod or a B. F. Skinner—books which are being used as texts in the local college or university. The Christian may write an open letter to local editors sounding an alarm about the evils of the book, demanding that it be removed from the curriculum of the university. This is particularly effective in cases of tax-supported education. The Christian can scream loudly that his personal rights are being violated. Anti-God secular religions are being taught at the university —and this evil thing is being done with tax monies paid by the Christians!

Many possible actions are open to the Christian. He can bring up a matter of concern for discussion in his Bible class. He can write a critical book review for a national campus publication. He can start a neighborhood discussion group. He can get a few friends together and launch a textbook evaluation service. He can make a fuss with the trustees of the local university or blast away at the state board of education. He can agitate, yell, scream, kick—all in a gentlemanly or ladylike manner, of course! The point is, go into action! The preacher will be delighted to have your help.

Mel and Norma Gabler, a Christian couple who are friends of the author and reside in Longview, Texas, became deeply concerned about educational materials being used in the local school system to reprogram the heads of their teenage youngsters. The Gablers made it their business to acquire, read, and analyze textbooks. Without any funding, and with little or no outside help, these Christian activists have fought the evils of secular humanism in the textbook scene all the way to the highest echelons of the state education department. They publish a small, inexpensive bulletin in which they release facts about textbooks in the state of Texas. These two parents, acting almost alone, have taken a stand for righteousness which has shaken the Texas State Education Department. In many instances the work of the Gablers has been highly successful; they have accomplished specific goals time and time again.

The struggle for righteousness is a·continuing war—not just

a battle. Godless interests are constantly seeking to insert evil establishments into many a local community—perhaps yours! Christians must be alert and vigilant, discerning not only the times but also the trends in the local community. We must be ready to jump into action almost on the spur of the moment.

GLORIFYING GOD

The *prerequisites* of Christian discernment are superlove and superknowledge. His *love* for his community neighbors will motivate the Christian to do all he can to protect them and their kids from evil influence. *Knowledge* of the local scene will complete his preparation for effective action. A Christian who loves his neighbors, and takes the trouble to acquaint himself with the social realities of his community, will soon get started in the exciting and rewarding work of practical righteousness.

The *practice* of Christian discernment involves the ability to distinguish between the things that differ—and to take appropriate Christian action.

The *products* of Christian discernment, or the results that will follow, are threefold. First, the Christian will be "sincere and blameless until the day of Christ" (Philippians 1:10). The original language conveys the idea of "not causing others to stumble." Second, the Christian will exhibit "the fruit of righteousness" (Philippians 1:11). This means right conduct —guided by God, properly placed, and effective. Third, the life-pattern of the Christian will result in "the glory and praise of God" (Philippians 1:11). The life of Christian discernment and action glorifies God. If it has no more justification than that it is eternally worthwhile.

James exhorts his readers: "But prove yourselves doers of the word, and not merely hearers who delude themselves"

(James 1:22). There are two kinds of deception—*satanic* deception and *self*-deception. Satanic deception is programmed into every phase of the life of man in this evil world-system. Self-deception is the state of those who think their Christianity will accomplish something worthwhile in the service of Christ, if they simply study the Bible, listen to sermons, and let the world float by.

In his little book entitled *Back to Freedom and Dignity* Dr. Francis Schaeffer says we have moved into a "post-Christian world." By this he means that Christian truth has ceased to be the guiding factor determining our way of life. Dr. Schaeffer pleads with Christians to recognize the implications of the crucial issues we face today, and to take the lead in giving direction to cultural change.

TWO CHOICES

We Christians have a big job to do. The fact that our Savior might return any day should not deter us from getting involved to the hilt in effective Christian action. We are expected to "occupy until He comes" (*see* Luke 19:13).

There are only two choices before us—Christian super-discernment and application on the one hand, or self-delusion, satanic superdeception, atrophy, retreat, and defeat on the other hand. Many Christians in Germany during the time of Hitler's rise to power chose the latter course. Which way will we go at this crucial hour in the history of our nation?

Closely related to the question of discernment is the issue of responsibility. Having discerned, we must act. God has handed over to Christians a very high level of responsibility to engage in practical works of righteousness as an outflow of faith. In the next chapter, we will amplify this line of truth.

7

Christians Are Responsible

Those who know and appreciate the Bible as the Word of God should be the first to practice the consistent application of its truths in all areas of life. This is the real meaning of Christian responsibility.

The Bible is the Word of God (2 Timothy 3:16). It reveals the will of God for man. It proclaims God's plan of the ages —the program to redeem fallen man through our Lord Jesus Christ. Its truths are all-encompassing, eternal, and adequate to meet our spiritual needs and guide us through life.

CHRISTIAN ACTION MUST FOLLOW FAITH

God is all-wise and He wants us to be guided by the words which He has spoken for our good. Generally speaking, the great doctrinal passages of the New Testament are followed by specific instruction for the guidance of our conduct. When God speaks, man is made responsible. Divine Revelation means human obligation. According to the Apostle James, Christians who are hearers only, and not doers of the Word, are self-deceived (*see* James 1:22). Christian action must follow genuine Christian faith. When God gives us something to believe, He also gives us something to do.

The eternal Scriptures provide us with highly practical guidance for decision, conduct, and action relative to our personal life and influence on others. This dimension of Christian application is frequently referred to as *Personal Christianity*. It is essential to effective Christian action. Until we allow the Savior to possess us in the depths of our personal experience, we will not be prepared to move forward into the many potential areas of Christian application.

Having appropriated Christ's person, we must apply His principles. Our responsibility extends beyond the doctrinal and personal dimensions of life to encompass every component of our life and culture. Our action must include all kinds of constructive influence designed to fulfill the will of God in all areas of life. The truth of God must be applied faithfully and consistently in order to influence the shaping of intellectual disciplines, human institutions, and the structures of society. The naming of disciplines like Applied Psychology, Applied Physics, Applied Mathematics, and so forth, suggests the propriety of referring to the action phase of our faith as Applied Christianity. For the consistent Believer, Christianity appropriated must always result in Christianity applied.

Applied Christianity is virtually unlimited as to its scope. It is concerned with such problem areas as marriage, parenthood, law and order in the community, economics, education, science, technology, the energy shortage, race relations, abortion, business operations, drug abuse, psychology, medicine, sex, pornography, obscenity, communications, criminology, penology, poverty, welfare, ecology, government, the meaning of freedom, occultism, war, the military draft, communism, socialism, capitalism, international relations, women's liberation, organized labor, and all other subjects which relate to the life of man on this earth.

Christian truth demands application throughout the entire range of the issues of life, from the most theoretical to the most practical. Applied Christianity is based on confidence in God's ability to improve the whole man through the redemptive work of our Lord Jesus Christ. The people of God—acting in harmony with the eternal purpose of God— are expected to accomplish the work of God in this world. To the degree that we perform in accordance with the will of God, we experience fulfillment and the problems of our society are solved.

THE BIBLE IS PRACTICAL

At one time or another all of us have heard the sentiment expressed that the only task of the Christian is to proclaim the Gospel, and that Believers who get sidetracked and involved in social issues just aren't serving Christ. In an effort to dispel the confusion relative to this controversial matter, let us give attention to the purpose of biblical Revelation itself.

The Bible is composed of a wonderful treasury of sixty-six different books. Only one of these—the Gospel of John—was written specifically to show men the way to heaven. According to John 20:31, this book was written in order ". . . that you may believe that Jesus is the Christ, the Son of God; and that believing you may have life in His name." This is the heart of the Gospel—the good news. Personal salvation is through the finished work of Christ on the Cross. It is available by the grace of God and is appropriated by faith alone.

The other sixty-five books of the Bible were written to provide the people of God with a wealth of instruction, guidance, and wisdom for the life they are living here and now on this earth. In the Old Testament the focus is on the nation Israel, its checkered experiences, blunders, triumphs. It is a time of preparation for the coming of the One who was the hope of all the prophets—the righteous Messiah-Savior.

The New Testament is largely made up of eyewitness accounts of His Coming, His life and teachings, His betrayal, Crucifixion, burial, and triumphant Resurrection. The balance of the New Testament records the history of the early Church and contains practical instruction for Christians living in a frequently hostile world.

Taken together, both Testaments provide an unfailing guide for Christian life and conduct. The Bible is both a road map to heaven and a manual for getting the most out of life during our experience in this world. It touches on the entire spectrum of human experience. Its appeal is to the whole individual, including his intellect, emotions, will, and conscience. The Bible brings God to man and man to God.

The Bible is a practical book. Either explicitly or implicitly, directly or indirectly, it provides a firm and reliable basis for every decision which we must make—in our personal life, our family life, our business life, our social life, our community life, our economic and political life. Familiarity with the principles, proverbs, and precepts contained in the Bible is the beginning of true understanding and genuine wisdom. It is the pathway to a wholesome appreciation of the meaning and purpose of life. It is the highway to happiness, strength, courage, inspiration, and achievement. Apart from the will of God as revealed in the Bible, all achievement is vain and ultimately meaningless. When our life is lived in harmony with the will of God, achievement is accompanied with vast benefits to ourself and to others.

APPLYING BIBLICAL TRUTH

Those who know and appreciate the Bible as the Word of God should be the first to practice and promote the consistent application of its principles and truths in all areas of life. Deriving our spiritual nourishment from our own private reading of the Bible and from the ministries of faithful teachers, we are obligated to apply biblical principles everywhere we go, and in all we do. The eternal truths contained in the Bible have vast meaning for all fields of concern.

Linder and Pierard have commented appropriately:

> It seems impossible to escape the logic of the argument that if we love our neighbors as ourselves, we will do what we can to improve their lives. This definitely will involve more than taking up an extra collection for the needy on Sunday morning or depositing a Christmas basket on the doorstep of some poor family. Sir Frederick Catherwood, an evangelical layman and former Director General of the National Economic Development Office of Great Britain, correctly suggests that a refusal to become involved in public affairs is a breach of the second great commandment (Mk. 12:31). According to Catherwood, "To try to improve society is not worldliness but love. To wash your hands of society is not love but worldliness."
>
> ROBERT D. LINDER and
> RICHARD V. PIERARD, *Politics*

A great deal of social concern, activity, and application should and will flow out from a genuine experience with Christ and a true apprehension of the Word of God. It is folly to say, as the advocates of the social gospel do, that we can redeem man by redeeming his society and influencing him externally. That is a reversal of the Gospel of Christ. On the other hand, there is much scriptural reason to question seriously the idea that those who have already appropriated the Savior should then limit their future walk to personal Christianity and evangelism, while neglecting the social area of man's life.

The Bible exhorts us to love one another, to love our neighbors, to honor and obey the magistrates, and to do good to all men. The implication seems to be that there is much room for social application. In fact, there is quite a body of New Testament revelation on this very subject.

FAITH AND CONSTRUCTIVE SERVICE

We must be careful to distinguish the true Gospel from the so-called social gospel. The true Gospel of Christ changes the evil heart of man through the application of the Blood of Christ and the power of the Holy Spirit, and man in turn changes his environment. The social gospel, on the other hand, is closely akin to the Marxist idea that we must manipulate the environment as a means of changing the inner life of man. Marx was an environmental determinist, whereas Christ was a spiritual determinist: "But seek first His kingdom and His righteousness; and all these things [material benefits] shall be added to you" (Matthew 6:33).

The social gospel is an unscriptural extreme in one direction, while a strict limitation of Christian responsibility to personal piety and verbal witness is an unscriptural extreme in another direction. The true Christian will recognize the primacy of redemption, and at the same time follow through with constructive service in all areas of life as an outflow of a redeemed heart. "For we are His workmanship, created in Christ Jesus for good works, which God prepared beforehand, that we should walk in them" (Ephesians 2:10).

It is interesting to note the "Lord of the harvest" exhortation in Matthew 9:38. In the immediate context of this famous missionary verse it is revealed that Jesus was "proclaiming the gospel of the kingdom, and healing *every kind of disease and every kind of sickness*" (verse 35, italics mine). The ministry of the Savior related regularly to the physical needs of men as well as to their spiritual needs. Again, when Jesus sent out the seventy as recorded in the tenth chapter of Luke, He included the instruction to "heal those . . . who are sick."

Granting the tremendous emphasis on evangelism throughout the New Testament, it is a grave error to conclude that it instructs us to engage in evangelism to the exclusion of the alleviation of the physical and temporal sufferings of men. God is pleased when we engage in those areas of ministry which relate to the physical, so long as our service flows out of redeemed and loving hearts.

Although the healing ministry of the Savior had the function of attesting His Messianic Person, He engaged in it basically because His divine heart of compassion prompted Him to do so. God wants His people to proclaim the Gospel and to be involved in helping people with the physical and temporal problems of life at the same time. As is widely recognized in foreign missionary work, such involvement will enhance the power and effectiveness of evangelism as people respond in a positive manner to the ministry of compassion.

The basis of Christian responsibility is the extensive body of divine revelation in both Testaments which provides the wide-ranging principles and the specific guidance upon which a stable and meaningful life, organization, or society may be constructed. There is room for differences of opinion as to how we may best act responsibly in a given situation of life. But there is no latitude for varying viewpoints as to the basic fact that God has made us responsible to act in accordance with our faith in Him and His Word.

> But someone may well say, "You have faith, and I have works; show me your faith without the works, and I will show you my faith by my works."
>
> James 2:18

Responsibility is the mainspring of influence. A responsible people, discerning the times and acting constructively in the power of God, will make an impact. Next we will see how influential we can and should be as Christians.

8

Christians Can Be Influential

Those who have been transformed by the power of Christ should exert an influence on others. A lack of influence betrays a lack of purpose, and a lack of purpose betrays a lack of genuine faith. Christianity unleashed is dynamite in any society. The only real hope for the future of our nation lies in the political activation of our Bible-believing citizens.

Although most Christians don't fully realize it, they can be very influential people. Furthermore, they *should* be. The purpose of this chapter is to point the way to greater influence within the community and the nation by those who are referred to by our Savior as the "salt of the earth" (Matthew 5:13).

Maintaining the doctrinal integrity of historic Christian faith, Christian citizens must exemplify in actual practice their commitment to biblical principles. This commitment must be sufficiently strong to motivate them, to shape their viewpoint, and to guide their conduct—not only in their personal lives—but also in their vocations, in their relationships to their communities, and in their leadership of various movements and organizations, small and large, within the nation. If Christians are to be influential, their faith must find fruition in worthy Christian action.

Christians must become recognized nationally for leadership in applying biblical principles to all of the complex and controversial issues confronting our society. Based on mature and competent analysis of these issues, they must always be ready with an answer to the question, "What guidance does the Bible give us on this matter?"

It is unfortunate that large numbers of Christians limit their practice of spirituality to the narrow limits of personal and family piety. Somehow they fail to conceive of spirituality in its broader application to all of the problems of life. Only when the spiritual message of the Word of God is made the determinative factor in guiding the thoughts of men toward the solution of major human problems, will real progress be made toward the building of a better society and a better nation. Here an attempt will be made to show how the Christian forces of our nation can exert a constructive influence by relating Christianity to ideology, church functions, education, business, and government.

CHRISTIAN ACTION AND IDEOLOGY

The prevailing spiritual climate within the society of men produces the ideology which rises to prominence and determines the direction of a civilization. An ideology is simply the complex of ideas, doctrines, and opinions which underlies and determines the shape and direction of the larger movements in the world. Even a peasant dictator like Mao-Tse-Tung was sufficiently intelligent to emphasize again and again in his "little red book" the crucial role of ideology.

Ideology is a way of thinking about human problems and how to solve them. There are only two basic ideologies—the ideology which is based on the will of God and the ideology known as "humanism," which is based on the will of man. Nothing is as vital to the best interests of a civilization as the maintenance of spiritual-ideological life in conformity with the will of God. When a divinely sanctioned ideology is the prevailing one, so that it gives shape to the institutions, economics, and government of a civilization, human service for God is maximized and the general well-being of a people is assured.

Christian citizens must become ideological leaders in the United States of America and in the Western world. Some of our Christian scholars have in the past half-century formulated the main elements of a unique and worthy Christian ideology which now needs to be expanded and related intelligently to all areas of life. To accomplish this, a series of ideological books should be prepared and distributed widely. They must be of sufficient stature to command the respect of the Christian community nationally, and of other citizens. These books should be extremely well researched and scholarly, yet readable and by all means practical.

A volume of suitable size should be devoted to each of several areas of concern which are identified as vital to the determination of the direction of our civilization. For example, a volume should be devoted to education, another to economics, another to law, another to government, another to business, another to the role of the Church, another to youth, and so forth. Such a series of writings can be effective in gaining respect for Christian ideology and extending its influence widely throughout our society and Western civilization.

CHRISTIAN ACTION AND THE CHURCH

The Church is one of the primary institutions established by God. It is founded on the apostles and prophets of the New Testament era, and our Lord Jesus Christ Himself is referred to as its "chief corner stone" (*see* Matthew 21:42). Conceived as the "body of Christ," all genuinely Christian individuals, organizations and movements are related integrally to the Church. In fact, it is highly doubtful if any Christian organization can attain its maximum usefulness to God and man unless its purpose and program relates in a meaningful way to the Church.

The typical local evangelical church today is doing a commendable work in the areas of preaching, Bible teaching, evangelism, and missions—but it has not developed successful methods of applying Christianity in the community. Much needed today are "service organizations" providing certain well defined services for the church—services which separately organized groups of Christians can provide for the church better than the church can provide them for itself. Adequate research and thought must be devoted to the determination of what services would fit into this category.

Services which are indispensable to the program of the church must be conceived, designed and launched. Possible programs might be: (1) Seminars for ministers on Christianity and social issues; (2) church-school courses on Applied Christianity designed for use in Sunday schools; (3) Christian liaison workers responsible for relating the church to the community and the community to the church; (4) Vocational testing and advisory service for young people in the churches. Ideally, it seems that all Christian service should flow out from the local church as the true New Testament institution established by Christ. There is no good reason why the Church should not, as it did in the last century, serve as the home base of nationwide action programs dedicated to the application of Christian principles in our society.

Christian application must be carried into many areas of life which have not traditionally been included within the program of the local church in this century. The training materials and programs developed through an active local congregation, small or large, can be published for utilization in churches across the land. The world has yet to see what God can do through a local church which so structures its membership that each individual will be required to be a "doer of the Word" and to assume a specific responsibility.

This responsibility may relate either to the internal functioning of the church or to the outreach of the church in the local community, the nation, or the world. In some instances, both internal and outreach responsibilities can be assumed and carried by the same individual. Every member of the congregation must be involved in the implementation and exemplification of biblical principles in the personal, ecclesiastical, and communal areas of human activity.

Imagine, for example, a special committee of the church involved in watching the proceedings in the local court and reporting these proceedings back to the local church and through the press and media to the larger community. Imagine a prayer meeting of the local church, in which a judge and jury involved in a criminal trial would become special objects of prayer by the people of God, with a view to the implementation of justice in accordance with biblical guidelines. Imagine another committee of the local church which would concern itself with moral conditions in the community; another which would concern itself with the office of the mayor and the city council, another with elected representatives to the state and national governments.

Why should not the specific problems of these elected officials be presented to the local congregation for prayer? Why should not a committee of the local church concern itself with a study of bills in the state and national legislatures? Biblical guidelines can be applied to the analysis of these bills, conclusions can be reached relative to the moral factors raised, and these conclusions can be transferred to the elected representatives. Explicit support of or opposition to such legislative proposals will not be necessary. Another committee of the church may relate itself to juvenile problems, another to penal institutions, another to the police department, another to educational institutions.

Under this concept, Bible teaching will be emphasized in the local church, but never merely as an end in itself. Such instruction must always lead to specific conclusions and applications in terms of the realities of the world in which we live. Evangelism and missions will be included in the program of the local church, but not to the exclusion of other vital areas requiring Christian application. True and genuine worship will also be emphasized, but such worship must not be regarded as the fulfillment of all Christian responsibility.

Properly conceived and operated, a church which will dare to apply Christian principles to a broad range of issues will become a blessing to the community and the nation. Applied Christianity could take the form of a dynamic and constructive new movement sweeping across the country, reflecting glory to God, and making a powerful impact on our society.

CHRISTIAN ACTION AND EDUCATION

The Christian school movement in America is already a growing cause. This is one of the most hopeful factors in American life today. Christians must develop ways and means of encouraging the Christian school movement on the elementary, secondary, and college levels. To some degree this has already been done through the publication of good articles on the Christian philosophy of education.

There is a great need for new Christian groups, which will dedicate themselves to the publication of vital textbooks and teachers' guides, and to the presentation of special seminars for Christian teachers. The purpose of such seminars might be to offer training in how Applied Christianity can be taught effectively in the classroom. On the college level, credit seminars should be offered for students, in cooperation with the administrative heads of various Christian colleges. These seminars might present the principles of Applied Christianity, with a view to encouraging students to enter public life and to maximize the utilization of Christian principles in the area of their chosen vocations.

There is probably no greater need in America today than the need for the teaching of Applied Christianity in our Christian schools. Abiding principles and moral values drawn from biblical sources must become the guidelines which give meaning and direction in the development of the principal fields of learning and activity. The student must be directed toward a comprehensive and integrated grasp of human knowledge—a total world view with God at the center.

The fundamental imperative of all ages is that man should look to God for guidance in all human affairs. This recognition is basic to the well-being of individuals, institutions, and nations alike. The founders of the American nation, who repeatedly invoked the Name of God when declaring their independence from old world tyranny, perceived the governing role of the Almighty. To exclude divine guidelines from the educational process is to move rapidly in the direction of a nightmare society such as those which have already enslaved masses of people in this century, under various forms of totalitarian government.

Large numbers of American citizens are aware of and concerned about the fact that our country has been undergoing a transformation from a theologically oriented society to an increasingly secularistic one in recent decades. The greatest need of the hour is for a return to recognition of divine authority and guidance. This is essential for the maintenance of a free, prosperous society. The very destiny of our nation might well be determined by our Christian schools.

Divinely revealed truth is basic, and the individual is primarily responsible to apply and observe it within his chosen vocation, whatever it may be. Social and economic problems are, at base, moral in nature. The key to the solution of our national dilemma lies in a practical application of the theological-moral guidelines within all areas of American life. A properly conceived Christian school will seek to fill the vacuum which has been created in secular educational institutions by the retreat from God and from rational concepts derived from God's Revelation to men.

The curriculum of such a school should feature theology as the parent discipline. From biblical theology should be drawn the basic principles and guidelines which will find application in each of the other fields to be included in the curriculum. Theological and biblical truth should be the integrating factor serving to fuse all disciplines into a realistic whole.

CHRISTIAN ACTION AND GOVERNMENT

A government is the administrative apparatus in control of a state. In the Western democratic republics a government is "in power" as a result of the will of a majority of the electorate participating in legally constituted elections. Properly speaking, the United States of America is a "state," as are the fifty different territorial units which comprise our nation. The state is a continuing institution ordained by God, and various governments may from time to time administer the affairs of state in harmony with a written constitution setting forth the principles and procedures on which the state is founded.

The key role of government in the lives of citizens is apparent. Through its legislative, executive, and judicial branches, the government of the United States controls, in a very large measure, the lives and destinies of our citizens. Boundaries are set on human behavior, laws are enforced, economic policies are determined, domestic and foreign affairs are administered. The life of the individual is largely circumscribed by the policies and practices of government. The fortunes of our citizens are to a large degree determined by the kind and character of government which holds power at a given time.

New Testament Christianity was born in the days of the Roman Empire, within territorial limits under the domination of the iron heel of Rome. So far as the masses of people were concerned, participatory government "of the people, by the people and for the people" was unthinkable. Under those circumstances, our Lord Jesus Christ and the writers of the New Testament Scriptures gave instruction that obedience should be rendered to government up to the point that the will of the state came into conflict with the will of

God, in which case primary obedience was owed to God. Thanks to the beneficial effects of Christianity in history, the democratic republics of the modern era were born, and the United States of America became the shining example of constitutionally guaranteed freedom for men within a free republic.

Representative government, which also might be referred to as "self-government," means that the people—all of the people who are of age and in good standing—have a voice in the government. In a real sense, they are a part of the government. They *are* the government. Not only may the people participate in the electoral process, but they may engage in educational and pressure group activities designed to affect the policies of government for better or for worse.

The biblically motivated people of this country, viewed collectively, make up a large segment of our population. It is most unfortunate that widespread lethargy and inactivity characterize the posture of the American Christian community in relation to government. By *default,* the Christian public has handed over the reins of government to the forces of secular humanism, immorality, and godlessness.

Masses of Americans have lost confidence in the integrity of government, and a mood of disillusionment has set in. Both of the two major political parties are widely regarded as lacking sufficient character to be worthy of occupying the place of power in this country. It is felt by many that our court system has become corrupt, and that many of the legislators whom the American people are sending to the state legislatures and to Washington lack the moral stature and competence which would qualify them to wield power in our government.

CHRISTIAN CHARACTER IN GOVERNMENT

The Apostle Paul exhorted the Thessalonian Christians to "always seek after that which is good for one another and for all men" (1 Thessalonians 5:15).

Goodness is compliance with the will of God in practical, everyday matters. Goodness in an individual tends to uplift and encourage those who are influenced by him.

Goodness can be enlarged and perpetuated through others, to the degree that one's circle of influence enlarges. Those whose goodness is evident in their own personal life and walk are constructively influential. Those who project goodness to their family, friends, neighbors, and business associates enjoy a wider sphere of constructive influence.

God wants His people to "do good to all men" (Galatians 6:10). Those who wish to fulfill this command have a great opportunity to do so through participation in government.

Local government should be in the hands of good men and women who have leadership ability. Only good people are able to make good decisions for the benefit of the community.

What is true in local government is true also in state and national government. Goodness in leaders means good decisions and good government. Good government is characterized by the administration of justice apart from favoritism at all levels. It derives its concept of justice from God, whose justice is inseparable from His love.

In recent years men have sought to establish a "Great Society" through political reform and welfare state practices. The effort failed because greatness is impossible apart from goodness. Today an increasing number of citizens are calling for the establishment of a *Good* Society. Is this possible?

Only if good people will elect good leaders who will render good decisions in the seat of power.

Where are the good people capable of serving as good leaders, and where are the good people capable of electing them? The greatest resource of goodness is to be found in that portion of our population which identifies with the God of goodness and desires to implement, in government and in our society, the principles of goodness which are inherent in His Word. Biblical faith is the essential mainspring of goodness. With it we will prevail; without it we will perish.

THE ONLY HOPE

There are literally millions of Americans who are committed to the major elements of biblical faith. They believe the Bible to be the Word of God, and they would like to see our nation guided by its eternal precepts. However, most of them are not actively applying those precepts in the life of the community and the nation. The only real hope for the future of our nation lies in the political activation of our Bible-believing citizens.

How can this be accomplished? It will not happen by itself. A determined effort must be made. Those Christians of all faiths, who perceive this need, must join in a carefully planned effort to persuade, train, and motivate other Christians to rise to the level of active participation in the civic affairs of our nation. The stakes are big. The survival of our freedoms, our finest institutions, and of our country itself is in the balance.

There's no such thing as a great *society* without great *people*. Individuals are the building blocks of any society. The society reflects what the people are. As we pointed out earlier, many of our most prominent leaders on the national scene are saying that our nation and our way of life are in jeopardy. What's the reason? It all boils down to the individual American and his moral values. It's a question of goodness at the grass roots.

The values on which this country was founded are no longer meaningful to large numbers of our citizens. Through the observance of those moral values, America became the greatest nation in history, with the largest measure of freedom and the highest standard of living ever known.

Now it is generally believed that the process of decay and decline has set in. Most Christians agree that this has resulted from a general renunciation of our spiritual-moral heritage. Too many Americans have turned away from the consistent practice of Judeo-Christian morals and conduct, which originally accounted for our national greatness.

The leaders of alien ideologies have much to say about *people power*. True people power lies in the moral dimension —in the character of the individual American who rears a family, obtains employment, or goes into business, and makes real decisions in real life—decisions which strengthen the moral fiber of our nation.

Every Christian citizen should be constructively dedicated to the upbuilding of his community and his nation. The time has come for the Christian public to awaken to its responsibilities in relation to government. Dedicated Christian citizens can have a significant role in bringing this about through programs such as the following:

1. Youth training seminars in Christianity and government
2. Publication of high-school and college textbooks on Christianity and government
3. Publication of bulletins, magazines, and journals in the area of Christianity and government

4. The training of volunteer Christian workers for government at the precinct level
5. Seminars on Christianity and government for elected officials
6. Pressure groups of various kinds designed to extend the Christian influence into many areas of concern relative to the moral life of the community and the nation
7. Utilization of radio, television, and the press for the projection of a Christian viewpoint relative to government and the issues confronting it.

CHRISTIANS AND COMMUNITY MORALS

Private-sector citizen action is almost always preferable to legislation when dealing with community morals. Sometimes both are needed. The legislative approach frequently raises the objection that so-called censorship amounts to a dangerous infringement of freedom. Direct citizen-group action, on the other hand, is both legitimate and highly effective—and it can often negotiate an end run around the censorship issue. Business interests which seek financial gain through the merchandising of pornographic films and literature can be brought to their knees by means of simple but effective Christian action on the local scene.

In the town of Victoria, Texas, a young minister, Neil Gallagher, has led an active campaign to rid his town of pornography. He organized a citizens-for-decency movement, recruited a couple of hundred citizens, and together they have restored a measure of decency to their town. They have removed X-rated films from the local theaters. They have been instrumental in the removal of pornographic magazines from the book racks of about two dozen stores and markets. Here is his story.

PORNOGRAPHY'S IN YOUR CITY TO STAY
IF YOU WANT IT. WE DIDN'T WANT IT.
by
Neil Gallagher

There are no X-rated movies in Victoria, Texas (population 56,000). There used to be. Seven nights a week. There are few Victoria stores with pornography on their shelves. There used to be twenty-six stores (drug stores, discount stores, book shops, and drive-in grocery stores) selling forty-eight pornographic magazines. God reaped a victory here. ("Victory in Victoria," *Christianity Today*, February 1, 1974, called it.) He'd been waiting a long time to do it. But He waits upon people. People are the channels of His power to claim His victories. If people sit, nothing's done.

Here's part of that story—a story that can be reenacted *anywhere*.

One day in November, 1973, amidst my book research (I was writing the first draft of a book on modern church history), the X-rated *Last Tango in Paris* came to our city (Victoria, Texas). X-rated movies had flourished here for years, but always at a distant drive-in theater. Their coming into the city's center bristled my indifference. Without breaking stride from research, I performed a minimal Christian and civic duty by swearing in a formal complaint to the district attorney. He told me I first needed to witness the movie.

I witnessed *Tango* and exploded. Supposedly an artistic movie, *Tango* projected—in bold color and unmistakable detail—the scenes and screams of breast and pubic nakedness, intercourse, and rape, available for adults or children to view. (The "X" and "R" movies, projecting tortured and lustful sex, are viewed by *children,* as well as adults.)

I shot petitions to fifty church and civic leaders asking for signatures demanding the expulsion of *Tango*. Hundreds of signatures ensued, were fired to the district attorney, and *Tango* left town. That was the beginning.

Having witnessed the screen's grotesque sex, I became convinced that most citizens simply *did not know* the contents of "X" and many "R" films, otherwise citizens clearly would not have allowed them to flourish. It was time to alert parents both to the contents of "X" and "R" movies and to the contents of porno magazines which *displayed the same grotesque sex as "X" and "R" movies* and which were sold in nearly every drug, food, and quick-stop store. A Christian friend, Tommy Clay, and I shopped around town buying samples of fifty porno magazines including the sex sophisticates, *Playboy, Penthouse, Venus,* and *Playgirl,* and so forth. The porno magazines, like "X" and "R" movies, displayed rape, intercourse, bestiality, oral intercourse, sex torture, child-molesting, and more. I then ran a notice in the city's largest paper stating that on such-and-such date and place there would be a meeting of all citizens interested in driving out pornography. Two hundred came. We laid out porno samples on long rows of tables; and after screening the audience for minors, we then instructed the audience to line up and file past the samples to inspect what was forced on their children from the shelves and screens of the city. (That strategy, incidentally, makes all the difference. The State of Rhode Island was cleaned up using the same strategy.)

We opened the meeting with a prayer and I spoke briefly to the group with these words:

Welcome fellow physicians. I address you as fellow physicians, because you are going to inspect cancer. Not because you enjoy it, but *hate* it. It will make you angry. Please channel your anger toward expelling pornography, just as Jesus Christ channeled His anger to expel money-sharks from a temple.

You have a choice. You may inspect this now, or wait until your children do. They can't help it. It's everywhere. Stores openly display it. Junior high through college students buy it or steal it to circulate at school. Eighty percent of movies project it, and television increasingly forces it before their eyes. Kids can't escape it. Legislation and civic indignation to stop the assault on children depends on us, not them.

Some people don't want you to inspect this. The pornographers. The pornographers want to continue to exploit our ignorance, and steal the money and minds of men.

The Supreme Court has consistently said that obscenity *is* illegal. Since June, 1973, it has also said that each community can determine what it allows *in its community*. Yet the pornographers have continued to violate both our existing law and community standards. What you will see tonight does not reflect the will of the people, but the will of pornographers. That will stop tonight.

But only if you hate pornography, as God hates it. And upon viewing the samples you will hate it with a fury you didn't know existed in you. You will hate it as a physician hates cancer.

They inspected the samples, and exploded. They took prepared petitions, gathered 1,000 signatures, and fired them into the hands of mayor, district attorney, city attorney, city councilmen, merchants and theater owners. We formed a local decency group (later aligning with *Citizens for Decency Through Law*), collected dues and ran newspaper ads describing the contents, error, and illegality of pornographic magazines and movies. We invited in for coffee small groups of neighbors, showing them samples of pornography, explaining that *their* kids were assaulted by this stuff. We appealed to the city's nuns, priests, and pastors to mobilize their congregations in one loud voice against pornography. We went on the radio. We met regularly (and still do—every second Thursday).

And God reaped a victory.

Ninety percent of stores removed pornography (including *Playboy*) from racks. All "X" movies left town. (Fourteen months later, they haven't returned.)

In Victoria both children and adults are now better protected from pornography. But not nearly as well as they are in the entire state of Rhode Island. Rhode Islanders employed the same *civic* efforts we did (including the strategy of showing samples discreetly), but added a powerful legal tool. They submitted to the legislature and had passed the clearest, toughest pornography law in the United States. The porno people challenged it in high courts and lost. The same law is now under consideration by our local city council in Victoria.

It's adaptable as a local ordinance, or state law. When in force in all fifty states, the porno racket will be decimated nationally. The man responsible for the law is Mr. Harold E. Doran, 1282 Newport Avenue, Pawtucket, Rhode Island 02860. He wants you to get in touch with him. You can write to me at 39 Milburn Road, East Providence, Rhode Island 02914. Get, read, and enact Rhode Island's Public Display Law in your community. It really works.

Another example of effective Christian action against pornography in a local community was reported by *Morality in Media* of New York. The account is reproduced here by permission.

The question is often asked, "I'm just one person. What can I do?"

What one person can do was dramatically demonstrated in New York City . . . .

On a Thursday morning early in February, thirty-year-old Manhattan stockbroker Stephen E. Shapiro and his wife were having breakfast in their spacious, terraced apartment. The apartment is located in the area media people invariably refer to as the "posh" Upper East Side. It also happens to be the area where Steve Shapiro was born and has lived all of this thirty-one years.

Steve and his wife were quietly going through the morning paper, when Steve threw down the paper in angry amazement. He had just seen an ad heralding the opening, the next day, of the sexploitation film *Deep Throat* at a theater right around the corner from his home.

Determination quickly replaced anger. Something had to be done. "You let this go," he later told reporters, "and what comes next? The hookers, the massage parlors, porno shops, peep shows. The line has to be drawn somewhere. It has to be drawn here."

But, how was the line to be drawn? Who would help? Steve began to think and then telephone. Calls to the Trans-Lux Theaters Corporation and Aquarius Releasing got him nowhere. Political figures? One could see nothing wrong with the film being shown in the area, another told him, "We're not interested in this sort of thing."

He noted that there were three Roman Catholic schools and one public grammar school in close proximity to the theater. On the way to his office he stopped at the offices of the New York Roman Catholic Archdiocese in midtown Manhattan. Officials there suggested he contact Morality in Media.

MM had one suggestion for Steve Shapiro—call a community meeting of a dozen or so representative people and determine how and to whom the community can express itself to have the film removed from the theater.

Steve took off that small launching pad, and at this writing had not yet splashed down . . . . He spent several hours Thursday afternoon telephoning pastors and rabbis, in addition to school principals and PTA officers. Almost without exception they agreed to meet at his home Friday afternoon or send representatives. The film was to open Friday at noon. Realizing that many at his meeting would be clergymen and women, Steve dashed down to Times Square Thursday night to view the film, so that he would be able to describe it. "I personally think the film is worse than any stag film."

All at his Friday afternoon meeting agreed, however, that whether or not the film was declared legally obscene was not the issue. It was still in litigation in New York County. The trial had ended, and the judge's decision was yet to be handed down.

"The arrogance of the people," said one clergyman, "to move it into a neighborhood theater before the judge even hands down a decision." The point at issue, the ad hoc committee decided, was a basic one: the neighborhood did not want the film playing there because of the danger it presented to the community. Steve Shapiro repeated, "What comes next?"

The committee, after considering several plans of action, settled on a concentrated petition campaign. Petitions gathered would be delivered to Trans-Lux officers. They would be in churches and synagogues in the area for congregations to sign that weekend, and signatures would be gathered wherever possible. Petitions said simply that signees believed the showing of the film to be "detrimental and dangerous to our community."

Steve Shapiro didn't wait. "I've never been an activist," he said, and swung into action. Early Saturday morning he called the local police precinct for permission to set up a table outside the theater. Before the theater opened, he had a sign tacked to a pole exhorting passersby to "Keep 'Deep Throat' Out of Our Neighborhood." Many of the people in the neighborhood were not yet even aware that the film had opened, and willingly signed. A little past noon, a local politician passed by and asked what he could do to help. Steve left him manning the table while he ran to telephone committee members to come help gather signatures on street corners in the area. As reinforcements arrived, he set up a second table outside the theater and then took off to make a few more signs.

By midafternoon, the campaign was in high gear; 1,000 signatures had already been obtained. The cast of characters that had gathered was interesting indeed. Looking out from the lobby was a vice-president of Trans-Lux Corporation. Standing on the sidewalk observing were the president of Aquarius and an attorney.

Early Sunday morning, the first sign of victory appeared. The foot-high words *Deep Throat* had disappeared from the sides of the marquee. Theater employees said the marquee was being "repainted."

Residents obtained 2,000 signatures on the street Saturday and Sunday. By Sunday night when petitions began to come in from churches the number rose to over 7,000. Petitions were still coming in to Steve Shapiro on Monday when he had a tip Trans-Lux was having a meeting. At the meeting's end, he telephoned and was informed the film would be pulled on Wednesday.

Trans-Lux officials denied that the decision came about as a result of community action.

They said they had pulled the film because they had another booking. A TV newscaster told Steve Shapiro off camera, "I don't buy that." Neither did Steve, who had conducted the campaign with a great deal of skill and reason.

In the usual confrontations which were inevitably to occur, *i.e.* "Who are you to determine what people can see or not see in this theater?" Steve Shapiro kept his cool: "A community has the right to say what it wants and what it doesn't want. This neighborhood does not want this film playing here."

One man or woman can set in motion a chain reaction which gets results. Both Neil Gallagher and Steve Shapiro proved it. In both cases direct action augmented by resolute demands for enforcement of existing laws proved highly effective. Christian action *can* improve community morals. In fact, the high motivation needed for such tasks is not likely to come from any source other than the Word of God.

CONCLUSION

While this chapter makes no pretense of being comprehensive, it does contain the results of some serious thinking concerning the role of the Christian citizen in the years ahead. It is sincerely hoped that further study, research, and analysis will be undertaken by other Christians, and that many additional forms of Christian action will be conceived and implemented. If this chapter serves the purpose of opening possibilities and encouraging Christian citizens to think constructively relative to their future role in American life, it will have served its purpose. Christians *can* be influential. They *must* be, if the shape of our civilization is to be determined by the Word of God.

Christians represent a powerful potential for constructive action in the community and in the nation. The consistent Christian exhibits a quality of "goodness" which fits him for such moral initiative. But are there enough Christians to swing the balance of power in the nation? Next we will take inventory of our Christian forces, with special reference to the possibility of impacting the country through Christian involvement in public leadership.

9

Assessing Our Christian Forces

Perhaps we Christians have failed to count our troops. There are many of us. If we have the courage to act in the power of God, the enemy will surely be overwhelmed.

In a free society of modern times, no single ruler holds the awesome powers of the absolute pagan monarch of ancient times. By virtue of a series of historical confrontations between the masses and the monarch, that power has been broken up into pieces, defused, and distributed widely among the citizens. Each citizen of voting age in the United States today, for example, wields a unit of political power. In a very real and tangible sense, the free citizen of today is a part of the ruling authority. He belongs to the power structure, in the nature of the case..He has no choice as to whether or not he should get involved in politics; he is already involved.

TWO KINDS OF CHRISTIAN CITIZEN

It might be helpful to identify two different groups of Christians in our country—those who believe a Christian should participate in the political system, and those who believe a Christian should not. Those who belong to the latter group generally hold the opinion that a Christian's only responsibility is to "live a Christian life," share the Gospel and study and teach the Bible. For the most part, these are sincere Christian people who are horrified at any thought that a Christian, who should be known for purity of life and example, should dive into the cesspool of politics. Large numbers of such Christian citizens even believe it is wrong for a Christian to vote. Others will go to the polls and vote when it is convenient to do so, but they refuse to carry their political influence any further.

It must be pointed out to these friends that every Christian in this country who is eighteen years of age or older is an active participant in the political system, whether he likes it or not. Those who piously claim that politics is not their business, and that a Christian should have nothing to do with it are actively supporting the rule of the godless. This, in turn, provides godless leadership with an opportunity to impose evils on our society, causing even Christians to do wrong. For example, when unprincipled measures are imposed through legislation, and Christians are taxed to support those measures, they are being forced to do wrong. According to Psalms 125:3 this is contrary to the will of God. As Edmund Burke (1729–97), that great Christian statesman of England, put it: "The only thing necessary for the triumph of evil is for good men to do nothing."

CHRISTIANS CAN IMPACT THE COUNTRY

Is there any hope that Christians can impact the country? Are there enough Christian-motivated citizens in the country to constitute an effective influence bloc? The answer is yes. Membership in all religious bodies has increased rapidly in the USA during this century. There are upwards of 100 million church members in the United States today. Many of these are of evangelical persuasion.

One of America's foremost authorities on the size and influence of the Evangelical Christian movement in America is the eminent theologian, scholar, philosopher, and author Dr. Carl F. H. Henry. I telephoned him at his home in Arlington, Virginia, on October 20, 1975, to ascertain his estimate of the numerical size of the total evangelical population of the United States.

Dr. Henry pointed out the difficulty of calculating the size of the evangelical community with precision. He stated that there is "no question" that the more theologically conservative churches are growing, while the liberal churches are experiencing a decline in membership. But the problem of calculating the number of conservative or evangelical Christians is complicated by the existence of so many loosely affiliated or wholly nonaffiliated churches, fellowships, Jesus groups, neighborhood prayer cells, home Bible studies, and so forth, widely scattered throughout the country.

A further complicating factor is the possibility that such churches, associations, and denominations as do state the size of their membership might err on the side of overstatement, on the average, by a margin of 5 to 10 percent.

Taking all variables into consideration and speaking cautiously, Dr. Henry estimated that "the number of Evangelical Christians in the United States might well run as high as 45 million at the present time." I believe Dr. Henry's estimate to be as reliable as any other that might be available; therefore for the purposes of this book I shall settle on 45 million as the total number of evangelicals in our country.

So we will proceed on the assumption that there are in the USA 45 million citizens who believe in God, in Jesus Christ, and the Bible, and who will accept the guidance of biblical principles once these are pointed out and clarified to them. Approximately 68 percent of these (or 30,600,000) are of voting age.

According to the Federal Election Commission in Washington, D.C., there were 173,223 political precincts in the United States as of November, 1972. Looking at potential manpower at the grass-roots level, based on our calculation of 30,600,000 Bible-respecting citizens of voting age, there are on the average about 177 of them in each of the 173,223 political precincts. This, incidentally, is where the real power is—not in Washington or in the state capitals, but right in the precincts where Christians live.

If denominational barriers are ignored (on the premise that the factors which unite Christians are greater than those which divide them), and if the entire Bible-respecting citizenry of the nation is taken into consideration, it appears that our Christian population nationally could—if properly trained—serve as a citizen bloc for the betterment of our political institutions and processes. This vast resource of Christian manpower is a sleeping giant which needs to be aroused. If this giant can be aroused and activated, at least the possibility exists that the tide of evil can be reversed and the deterioration of our civilization arrested.

THE PRINCIPLE OF MINORITY RULE

If Christians are to be inspired by a reasonable hope that they can make a favorable and healthy impact on the country, they must understand the principle of minority rule. This simply means that a minority of citizens, and not a majority, have effective control of a country. This principle is applicable to all nations throughout all time.

In volume II of his book series entitled *Modern Democracies* (Macmillan, 1921) Lord James Bryce gave us a classic statement on minority rule:

> In all assemblies and groups and organized bodies of men, from a nation down to the committee of a club, direction and decisions rest in the hands of a small percentage, less and less in proportion to the larger and larger size of the body, till in a great population it becomes an infinitesimally small proportion of the whole number. This is and always has been true of all forms of government, though in different degrees (p. 542).

The most extreme form of minority rule is the absolute monarchy—the rule of one person. At the other end of the spectrum is the democratic republic of modern times in which all adult citizens, with the exception of a few criminals, enjoy the right to vote.

Even though the vote of the majority decides an election, it would be a mistake to conclude that in reality the majority actually rules. The fact is that an active minority will always rule over a passive majority.

Most leaders of organizations, including pastors and politicians, will agree that active volunteer leadership does not constitute more than something between 5 percent and 10 percent of total participants. Taking 5 percent as the basis of calculation, 1.5 million people can influence significantly the voting of 30,600,000 God-centered citizens. Taking 10 percent as the basis of calculation, 3 million people can serve as a spearhead of influence within the same God-oriented group. If this were to happen, of course, the 30,600,000 biblically guided citizens might well spearhead a sizeable influence upon the larger electorate within the nation. One trained and dedicated Christian leader in a precinct of 250 to 1,000 voting adults, bolstered by the assistance of a few other properly trained and active Christian citizens, and working within the guidelines of an intelligent strategy, can prevail for his political party and cause. Qualified Christian candidates *can* be identified and elected to public offices at all levels.

If they are willing to become intelligently active as a force for God, Christians can assure the rule of the righteous —the rule of those whose philosophy of government, policies, and actions will be guided by eternal principles derived from God, rather than by shallow humanism and expediency. In order to accomplish these goals, a worthy and effective strategy or method is needed. In Part III are suggested program guidelines. A basic biblical principle of strategy will be presented next.

PART III

The Program

Decades go by, and the scars and sores of the past are healing over for good. In the course of this period some of the islands of the Archipelago have shuddered and dissolved and the polar sea of oblivion rolls over them. And someday in the future, this Archipelago, its air, and the bones of its inhabitants, frozen in a lens of ice, will be discovered by our descendants like some improbable salamander.

ALEXANDER SOLZHENITSYN
The Gulag Archipelago

The Christian resources of the United States must be marshalled, focused, and directed toward the solution of our problems. In order to influence the direction of this nation, Christian resources must be directed primarily toward the development of biblically guided Christian public and political leadership. Christians must occupy many of the positions in which key decisions are made. Christian leadership must be developed for the legislative, executive, and judicial branches of government at all levels.

10

God's Method: Going
to the Center of Power

Where will the decision be made? Let's find out and go there.
Perhaps we can do more good in less time. This is God's
method.

Our civilization is in decline. All the wisdom and power of
man is helpless to solve this problem. But God is able to take
a hand in the affairs of this nation. He wants to turn the tide.
He wants to do this through His people. He will do it as
soon as we get in step with Him and develop a worthy
Christian program of action that is consistent with the guidelines which He has given us in His Word. Let's begin to
think about such a program of action in this chapter.

A THEME VERSE

First, let's select a theme verse from the treasury of the
Scriptures—a verse that will provide guidance and motivation. From among the many possibilities we like Psalms
125:3—an almost forgotten expression of God's will. A clear
understanding of this verse may be enhanced by taking note
of more than one translation:

For the rod of the wicked shall not rest upon the lot of the righteous; lest the righteous put forth their hands unto iniquity.

KJV

For the scepter of wickedness shall not rest upon the land of the righteous; That the righteous may not put forth their hands to do wrong.

While he has not translated as literally as the King James and the New American Standard Bible, Kenneth Taylor in his Living Bible has gone to the heart of the meaning of this verse:

For the wicked shall not rule the godly, lest the godly be forced to do wrong.

This great verse expresses an abiding principle of God's will. His care for nations is clearly expressed in the fact that He doesn't want the wicked to occupy the place of power. That would be contrary to His holy nature, since it would result in the doing of evil by godly people. Of course, nations which repudiate the rule of God have many times in the past been placed under the rule of "the basest of men" (Daniel 4:17 KJV) as a means of judgment. But the rulership of the wicked over the godly is contrary to the perfect will of God.

RULERSHIP RESPONSIBILITY

Since this is the case, it follows that God has given His own people a responsibility in the area of rulership. Since the rule of the wicked is contrary to His will, it is clear that God's program for communities and nations calls for the rule of godly citizens. God must be highly displeased with the all-too-common refrain "politics is dirty." He must be even more displeased with the carelessness, lethargy, and inactivity which characterize the lives of so many Christians who repeat that slogan so frequently.

God does want to bless human societies. God does detest rottenness in high places (*see* Isaiah 1:5, 6). God is the center of all power in this universe. Righteousness does exalt a nation (*see* Proverbs 14:34). God does want his people to exert a mighty influence in the life of a nation. They *can*, if they are willing to follow His plan.

As we read the Bible we become aware that God has a plan for His people, and that He has presented it with great clarity. The main feature of it is that God sends His people to the center of power. In the third chapter of Exodus, the plight of God's people is described in words like *affliction*, *sorrows* and *oppression*. They were reduced to a grinding drudgery under the heels of the Egyptian slavemasters. The outlook was bleak in the extreme. God's people had no army, no weapons, and no leadership. Standing in the pathway of any possible escape was an insurmountable geographical barrier—the Red Sea. But with God, for whom all things are possible, the outlook was bright. "So I have come down to deliver them from the power of the Egyptians," said the Lord (Exodus 3:8)

GOD USES A MAN

Although God was about to commit His own unlimited power to the cause of delivering the Israelites, His program involved the agency of a man. There is the familiar account of the "burning bush," from which God spoke to Moses and announced, "I will send you to Pharaoh" (Exodus 3:10).

It is curious but nevertheless true that God chooses to use men for the accomplishment of His purposes. Five times it is recorded in the early chapters of Exodus that the Almighty God issues a direct command to a weak, vacillating man— the command to *go*. Not only does God issue the command to *go*, but He also gives Moses the content of the message to be delivered to the mightiest monarch on earth:

> "Then you shall say to Pharaoh, 'Thus says the Lord, "Israel is My son, My first-born. So I said to you, 'Let My son go, that he may serve Me'; but you have refused to let him go. Behold, I will kill your son, your first-born." ' "
>
> Exodus 4:22, 23

From his own standpoint, Moses raises two valid objections: "They won't believe me" (*see* Exodus 4:1) and "I am not eloquent" (*see* Exodus 4:10). We might refer to the first objection as the *confidence gap* and to the second as the *communications gap*. Indeed there is a human problem involved in attempting to get a message across to the godless. The secular mind, the scientific mind, and the statist mind are not generally open to the will of God. Nevertheless, God's command is to *go*. As in the days of Moses, God will take care of the objections of the godless.

GOD-DIRECTED DIPLOMACY

God's method of impacting a nation is to select a man, give him a message and send him to the center of power. Although Pharaoh Thutmose III (1432 to 1450 B.C.) was one of the mightiest rulers of the ancient world, God's man with God's message, backed up with God's power, prevailed. The result was deliverance from bondage as recorded in the twelfth chapter of Exodus. Although the burning bush experience of Moses has been the basis of many a missionary and evangelistic challenge, notice that the voice of the Lord from the fire launched Moses on a mission which was basically *political* rather than religious or spiritual. Although Pharaoh was staunchly committed to the service of Satan, Moses was not told to go down to Egypt and convert the heathen monarch. Moses' mission involved God-directed diplomacy in the court of Pharaoh.

OTHERS SENT TO THE POWER CENTER

God's method has frequently been that of sending His chosen servants to the center of power. This was true in the days of the Judges. This was true in the days of Queen Esther, who in her effort to save the Jewish population from genocide under the wicked Haman, went directly to King Ahasuerus saying, ". . . if I perish, I perish" (Esther 4:16). After Isaiah's great vision of the Lord in the temple (Isaiah 6:1–8), the prophet was commissioned by God to "go out now to meet Ahaz" (Isaiah 7:3) and to deliver a special message to him. It was a *political* mission.

In the providence of God, the Prophet Daniel was sent on a political mission to the great King Nebuchadnezzar. The activities of most of the prophets, as well as those of Ezra and Nehemiah, Saul, David, Solomon, and most of the Old Testament personalities, were highly *political* in nature.

The ministry of the Lord Jesus Christ was widely perceived as being highly political in the context of pagan, totalitarian Rome. Although His followers identified with His spiritual purposes, He did become a highly significant and visible figure on the *political* scene of those times. His Crucifixion took place in a setting of mounting hostility on the part of the religious and political leadership. His messianic claim was perceived as a threat to the Jewish rulers (Luke 22:66–71), who accused Him before Pilate, the Roman

Governor of Judea (Luke 23:1, 2). The charges that He had forbidden the payment of tribute to Rome, usurped the royal title, and perverted the nation were *political* in nature. His life and ministry were out of harmony with the *political* forces of pagan Rome.

Paul the Apostle appeared before Governor Felix, and made his defense before King Agrippa (Acts 26). When his citizenship rights were denied, Paul announced, "I appeal to Caesar" (Acts 25:11). Later, through the influence of Paul, a Christian church is born in Caesar's household. Although the appeal to Caesar was motivated by legal-political considerations, it opened a strategic door for the evangelization of people who stood at the center of power in the empire. Whether for purely political reasons, or for evangelistic reasons, going to the center of power is God's method.

How can Christians go to the center of power today? By moving into positions of public leadership so that the wicked will not continue to rule over us, causing us to do evil. This does not mean that every Christian should become a candidate for public office. It does mean that every Christian should become politically active at some level. The possibilities range from calling on neighbors in the local precinct, to becoming a candidate for the presidency of the United States. Pressure group activities are tremendously important and can be effective. More about this later. For the moment it is important to understand that the Christian citizen living in a democratic republic does have a responsibility to make his influence felt through the political system. Our mandate is clear. Whether in the local community, the county, the state, or the nation at large, Christians must carry their influence to the very center of power, and their influence must express itself both in spiritual ministry and in practical and realistic political programs.

Having discovered the biblical principle of going to the center of power, let's see what this implies for the Christian living in a democratic republic today. We turn now to the question of the development of a Christian strategy for impacting our society.

11

Developing Christian Strategy

In order to influence the direction of our nation, Christian public and political leadership must be developed. Specific training programs, aimed at the "Christian grass roots," must be launched.

Some Christians believe the leadership of the Holy Spirit in the Christian life means that planning and strategy are unnecessary. But most of those who voice this opinion engage in strategy-planning in their business life, in their personal financial affairs, in their family life, and in other areas. The Bible is not opposed to God-directed strategy; it is opposed to humanistic strategy which is developed outside the will of God.

The greatest strategist of all is the Lord Himself. His age-long plan of redemption, culminating in the judgment of the wicked and in the triumph of His righteous cause, is itself reflective of a great "strategy." There is much evidence of strategy in the ministry of Christ and in the missionary activities of the Apostle Paul.

CHRISTIAN STRATEGY AND THE WILL OF GOD

In certain instances, as in 1 Corinthians 9:19-23, the strategy of the great apostle is stated explicitly. In this passage, Paul called attention to his principle of cultural adaptation to the group which he was seeking to reach with the Gospel. "To the Jews I became as a Jew," he explained. A rapid reading of the book of Acts is sufficient to remind us that Paul almost always went first to the Jewish synagogue in a community to which he sought to take the Gospel. Why? Because God led him to do so. It was God's purpose, God's will, God's strategy. Paul the Apostle was simply lining up with the will of God and following a strategy which, he was assured, came from God. "I have become all things to all men," he explained, "that I may by all means save some."

The Apostle Paul believed that he had received very specific divine leading for his ministry. It is important for us today to act on the same conviction. Although God does not hand us His will for the specific activities of life written on a sheet of paper and enclosed in a sealed envelope, He still directs His people. The guiding principles have already been written down in the Word of God, and Christians are responsible to act on them.

As far as specific divine leadership is concerned, most Christians will agree with the late Dr. Lewis Sperry Chafer, founder of Dallas Theological Seminary, who reminded his students frequently, "God can speak loudly enough to make a willing soul hear." This is a good maxim to keep in mind in all that we do—even in the development of a strategy for Christians. "For all who are being led by the Spirit of God, these are sons of God" (Romans 8:14). Much planning can take place without the necessity to cite chapter and verse from the Bible for support. But all Christian planning must take place within the framework of the principles and truths revealed in the Word of God. The Holy Spirit never leads one to do that which is contrary to the written Word.

Sometimes there is disagreement between Christians as to the interpretation of biblical guidance for specific issues, but generally an area of harmony can be established if the God-ordained principle of seeking the counsel of others is observed. ". . . But a wise man is he who listens to counsel" (Proverbs 12:15). ". . . And in abundance of counselors there is victory" (Proverbs 24:6). Any group of Christians who truly desire to find the will of God, and are willing to submit to His direction, can identify sufficiently wide areas of agreement to justify cooperative action.

THE NEED FOR PRACTICAL TRAINING

A major purpose of this book is to call upon Christians everywhere to identify with the goal of developing a viable program to activate Christians in the effective exercise of their citizenship responsibility, to the end that biblical principles shall guide the affairs of the nation. If this goal is to be reached, it will be necessary to develop effective training programs. Christian citizens must be trained and motivated to become active, informed voters who are willing to work for and contribute financially to the support of worthy candidates. Christian voters of all political parties must be taught how to apply biblical principles for decision-making in the electoral process. Qualified Christians must be encouraged to become candidates for public office. Members of the Christian public must be taught how to undergird the Christian public leader once he has gained office. If Christians are to become effective political workers, they must be shown how. Political propaganda and ballyhoo can never take the place of practical training in the noble art of public influence.

Any enduring change in our nation and its institutions must be brought about through the continued proclamation of the Gospel of Christ, followed up with the consistent application of Christian principles. The Christian resources of the United States must be marshalled, focused, and directed toward the solution of America's problems. And we must remember that although many of our problems are *national,* their solution is generally *local.* The changes which must be made in our society simply cannot and will not be made apart from the active participation of Christians in the decision-making process in the local communities in which they reside.

This means that Christians must occupy more of the positions in which key decisions are made. Christian leadership must be developed for government at all levels, from the local school board to the United States Congress. In order to develop such leadership, it is necessary to offer biblically based positive training programs to potential leaders within the Christian community.

A PRACTICAL TRAINING PROGRAM
FOR OUR TIME

God has graciously given, for the good of man, three basic institutions:

1. *The Family* (Genesis 2:18, 21–25; Ephesians 5:21–33)
2. *The Church* (Matthew 16:18; Acts 2 through 28; Letters of Paul)

3. *The Nation* (Genesis 10; Deuteronomy 32:8; Jeremiah
    46:17–26; Daniel 4:17, 25, 32, 34–37; 5:25–31; Acts
    17:26; Romans 13:1–7; 1 Timothy 2:1–4; 1 Peter 2:
    13–17)

God has revealed His will for each of these three institutions, and to the degree that men are obedient in each sphere
the good of the people of God and of the entire society is
served.

The Church is responsible not only to evangelize, teach
doctrine, and minister to the personal needs of Christians,
but also to teach them how to *serve* Christ effectively within
the family, the church, and the nation.

Numerous churches and service organizations offer excellent seminars and other training programs on youth conflicts,
church growth, marriage and the family, witnessing, teaching, preaching, and serving Christ through personal ministry
and conduct in the family and the local church.

Little or no instruction is available, however, through the
local church or Christian service agencies, to train members
in the all-important matter of serving Christ through effective public leadership within the community and the nation.
This type of practical leadership training is sadly lacking and
desperately needed.

Our local churches must have a vital role in any program
to change the direction of our society. Properly conceived,
the local church can and should be tremendously effective
in exerting a righteous influence in the community. In a
certain sense, and without abandoning its spiritual ministry,
the church can include in its program leadership training
and "pressure-group activities" dedicated to the glory of God
and the well-being of the citizens. In the next chapter sug-
gestions will be given as to how this can be done.

12

The Church
of Applied Christianity

*God's great plan for the Church is that it shall minister to
His people and, through them, to the whole world. He wants
the Church to be a channel of blessing everywhere, always.
To fail to find and follow His plan is to fail God in the fulfillment of His far-reaching purpose. The focus of most church
programs is Bible teaching and worship. These are all-
important, but incomplete unless action follows.*

Most pastors are well aware of the fact that the Church
could use some improvement in terms of impact-effectiveness.
The purpose of this chapter is to explore possibilities and in
this way to stimulate constructive thought, discussion, and
planning, to the end that the Church may once again become
an effective force in our society as it was earlier in our history. Let's sketch a profile of a proposed faith-and-action
Church for our time under the ficticious name *Church of
Applied Christianity.*

BALANCING FAITH WITH ACTION

Doctrinally, the suggested Church of Applied Christianity,
which I am describing, stands in the mainstream of historic

Christianity. In practical matters, it seeks to balance faith with suitable Christian action. It provides for Bible study, worship, and fellowship, just as most churches do. These legitimately Christian activities, however, are never ends in themselves. Always they must result in real Christian action designed to deal effectively with real problems in the real world of today. Such action will be preventive, developmental, and corrective in nature. Inevitably it will stimulate individual Christian growth, and lead to a healthy acceleration of church growth.

The Church of Applied Christianity directs Christian action to all of the problem areas of life, whether personal, institutional, national, or international in scope. No area of life is outside the interest of the Christians who belong to this church. They believe the truth of God must be applied universally—that it must relate in a meaningful way to law, medicine, economics, agriculture, communications, business, politics, technology, education, welfare, psychology, and the arts, as well as to the personal dimension of life.

In addition to being a legal, corporate organization recognized by the laws of our land, the Church is a spiritual *body* with Jesus Christ Himself as its *Head* (*see* Ephesians 1:22, 4:15). Conceived as the *body of Christ*, all genuinely Christian individuals belong to the Church. In this sense it is a dynamic, thriving organism. It is an active group of people who are daily living, working, playing, studying, investing, traveling, communicating, leading, following, and so forth, in the home, neighborhood, community, nation, and world. The Bible directs a large body of instruction and exhortation to the Church in this sense. It refers to *Christians* as the "salt of the earth" and as the "light of the world" (Matthew 5:13, 14)—figures of speech which suggest moral purity, preservation of values, constructive influence, and enlightened leadership.

The letter of James stresses the fact that God requires the practical application of Christian faith. "[Be] doers of the word and not merely hearers who delude themselves," wrote James (1:22). Professing Christians who feel that "going to church" fulfills their Christian obligations are self-deceived or, to translate differently, self-deluded. Their delusion arises from the fact that they regard themselves as living in a manner pleasing to God, while in fact they are not.

Some of the practical areas of Christian application cited by James are: providing for orphans, caring for widows, showing mercy, supplying clothing, food and shelter, business and financial management, aiding labor relations, alleviation of suffering. These are obviously real human problems. God expects His people to direct their resources and energies toward the solution of these and a host of other pressing problems in the everyday lives of their neighbors and fellow citizens.

EVERY MEMBER A DOER

The Church of Applied Christianity is unique in that it carries Christianity into many areas of life which are not normally included within the vision and program of traditional churches. In fact, a requirement of membership is that the individual must be a "doer of the Word." He must assume a continuing responsibility, consistent with his gifts and interests, in some needy area of Christian application. He must also work with others in a serious effort to train and involve others in a grand Christian program designed to "do good to all men" (Galatians 6:10).

Every member of the Church of Applied Christianity will

be involved in the implementation of biblical-Christian principles, not merely within the narrow confines of personal piety, but in one or more areas of practical expression as well. No member of this church suffers from that type of "spiritual indigestion" which afflicts those who are constantly exposed to the teaching of the Word, yet are deprived of the encouragement and instruction necessary to practice its precepts in an effective manner.

The Church of Applied Christianity is involved, first of all, in action designed to *prevent* certain evils from befalling the youth and other citizens residing in the local and national community. Drug and crime prevention are examples of this type of activity. A second category of action is *developmental* in nature. It is concerned with constructive approaches to the implementation of Christian truth within the institutions of our society, including government. It seeks to bring about improvement at all levels. The third type of Christian action is basically *corrective.* It is directed toward clearly recognized existing moral and social ills which are detrimental to our neighbors, their children, and members of the larger national community. It seeks to solve existing problems.

ACTION GROUP OUTREACH

A considerable number of Christian action groups move out into the community from the Church of Applied Christianity. These groups are not the church itself; they are, however, composed of members and friends of the church who wish to form associations, committees, and various types of groups dedicated explicitly to the application of Christianity. They meet regularly to study the Word of God, formulate action programs and carry them out in a manner consistent with biblically recognized guidelines. Here is a partial list of these action groups, together with brief descriptions of their essential functions.

- **Christian Evangelistic Action Group.** Function: Planning and implementing evangelistic projects and campaigns in the local community.
- **Christian Missionary Action Group.** Function: Planning and implementing evangelistic and other appropriate projects outside the local community, including foreign countries.
- **Christian Community Action Group.** Function: Study the needs of the local community, and develop appropriate Christian programs designed to solve community problems.
- **Christian Educational Action Group.** Function: Develop and execute programs designed to improve the moral and intellectual climate of the public schools in the local community, and plan the launching of private Christian schools whenever and wherever possible.
- **Christian Correctional Action Group.** Function: To study all correctional and penal institutions in the local community, with a view to implementing such improvements as may be suggested by genuine Christian concern.
- **Christian Law Enforcement Group.** Function: Study ways and means of supplementing the services of all law enforcement agencies, with a view to contributing toward the maintenance of order and tranquility in the local community.
- **Christian Court Services Group.** Function: Watch and report to the public on the activities of all local courts, taking special note of specific instances in which the principles of Christian justice are violated. Encourage the administration of impartial justice.

- **Christian Legal Action Group.** Function: Develop Christian legal programs designed to utilize the process of law for the enhancement of worthy Christian goals in society.
- **Christian Political Action Group.** Function: Inform the public of Christian perspective on controversial and key issues confronting the community and the nation. Identify potential Christian political candidates, encourage them to run for public office, help them to gain election and undergird them throughout their term of service.
- **Christian Legislative Action Group.** Function: Provide Christian analysis of key bills before city, county, state, and national legislative bodies, reporting a clearly stated Christian position to the community through the press and other available media.
- **Christian Cultural Action Group.** Function: Study the most effective means of bringing Christian influence to bear on the cultural life of the local community, and implement programs designed to do so.
- **Christian Moral Action Group.** Function: Develop and maintain an ongoing program to apply Christian values in such a manner as to enhance the moral climate and life of the local community.
- **Christian Social Action Group.** Function: Marshall the Christian resources of the community with a view to reducing poverty, alleviating suffering and caring for the needy in a manner which will encourage self-help and the attainment of financial self-sufficiency.
- **Christian Business Action Group.** Function: Encourage the practice of Christian principles in business. Train youth in successful methods of business operation. Provide business opportunities for Christian investors and entrepreneurs.
- **Christian Scientific Action Group.** Function: Encourage scientific research and investigation by Christians, with a

view to combating disease and harnessing available energy
for the enhancement of the quality of life of all citizens.

- **Christian Economic Action Group.** Function: Provide
Christian perspective on economic issues confronting the
community and the nation, and develop appropriate Christian action designed to solve economic problems.
- **Christian Research Group.** Function: Marshall the resources of the foremost Christian research personnel and
facilities, with a view to providing reliable information
regularly to the press and other communications media.
- **Christian Media Action Group.** Function: Develop and
implement a total strategy for maximum Christian utilization of the public media, with a view to influencing our
communities and our country through the faithful application of Christian principles.
- **Christian Leadership Action Group.** Function: Train youth
and other interested citizens in the effective utilization of
Christian leadership principles, with a view to placing
responsible Christian leaders in key positions in the nation.
- **Christian Publishing Group.** Function: Publish, through
the medium of a Christian weekly paper, the findings,
activities, and recommendations of all other groups associated with the Church of Applied Christianity.

GOD WANTS PARTICIPANTS

The Church of Applied Christianity is based on the premise that the segregation of Christian faith from biblically
guided Christian action is not the way to live a life pleasing
to God. The mere enjoyment of personal piety is not the
Christian life. God has ordained that His people should be
workers—that they should participate in the fulfillment of
His great commission to "subdue the earth" (Genesis 1:28),

as well as in His great commission to "make disciples" (Matthew 28:19).

What is the current status of the Church of Applied Christianity? Fortunately, many fine churches are already involved, to some degree at least, in the application of Christianity within the community in accordance with the concept presented here. But to our knowledge, no church answering fully to these specifications has yet been established in our time. When will such a church ever become an established reality? Only when at least a handful of Christians in some community get together and form a church which meets these unique qualifications. The need for change is dramatically evident. Given the leading and power of God in the lives of a few adventurous Christians who dare to be different, a Church of Applied Christianity can indeed become a reality in American life. By all means it should.

If and when such a church is organized, those who join it will become pioneers in one of the most Christ-honoring and imaginative programs of all the centuries since our Lord Jesus Christ founded the Church.

CONCLUSION

Let Us Cross Over

⁶ Then Jonathan said to the young man who was carrying his armor, "Come and let us cross over to the garrison of these uncircumcised; perhaps the Lord will work for us, for the Lord is not restrained to save by many or by few."

⁷ And his armor bearer said to him, "Do all that is in your heart; turn yourself, and here I am with you according to your desire."

⁸ Then Jonathan said, "Behold, we will cross over to the men and reveal ourselves to them.

⁹ "If they say to us, 'Wait until we come to you'; then we will stand in our place and not go up to them.

¹⁰ "But if they say, 'Come up to us,' then we will go up, for the Lord has given them into our hands; and this shall be the sign to us."

¹¹ And when both of them revealed themselves to the garrison of the Philistines, the Philistines said, "Behold, Hebrews are coming out of the holes where they have hidden themselves."

¹² So the men of the garrison hailed Jonathan and his armor bearer and said, "Come up to us and we will tell you something." And Jonathan said to his armor bearer, "Come up after me, for the Lord has given them into the hands of Israel."

¹³ Then Jonathan climbed up on his hands and feet, with his armor bearer behind him; and they fell before Jonathan, and his armor bearer put some to death after him.

¹⁴ And that first slaughter which Jonathan and his armor bearer made was about twenty men within about half a furrow in an acre of land.

¹⁵ And there was a trembling in the camp, in the field, and among all the people. Even the garrison and the raiders trembled, and the earth quaked so that it became a great trembling.

¹⁶ Now Saul's watchmen in Gibeah of Benjamin looked, and behold, the multitude melted away; and they went here and there.

1 Samuel 14:6–16

13

Wanted: Stouthearted Christians

The day of battle has arrived. God has brought us to this time for a great purpose. Let us wage war against those evil forces which threaten to consume our children, our neighbors, our land.

It is a dark day in Israel. The Philistines, a powerful sea people to the West, have launched a three-pronged assault against the heartland of the kingdom of Saul. The military odds are overwhelming in favor of the invaders—six thousand horsemen, thirty thousand chariots and "people like the sand which is on the seashore" (1 Samuel 13:5).

In the face of this onslaught, terror has struck the people of Israel, who hide themselves "in caves, in thickets, in cliffs, in cellars, and in pits" (1 Samuel 13:6). In order to escape the coming cloud of war, many of the Hebrews have already fled across the river Jordan to the East, finding safety in the land of Gilead.

Those who remain in the invaded territory follow a morally bankrupt Saul with fear and trembling. No wonder, for a census has revealed that a ragtag army of only six hundred men faces the Philistine scourge—and the Philistine garrison is now in the pass of Michmash, in place for the final thrust at the jugular of Israel.

Is the end at hand for the people of God? Will the off-spring of Abraham be crushed out of existence by the Satan-worshipers of Gaza, Ekron, and Ashdod? Will those whom God once established be erased from the earth? Will the inheritors of Canaan be wiped from the memory of history? Will the genealogical line of the promised Messiah be broken forever in the hurricane of blood and dust about to sweep over the land? Will the dark day of Israel's demise spread out to engulf a languishing world that desperately needs the light of salvation? The hour is at hand when the issue of life or death must be resolved—for Israel and the world.

In a reflective mood as he peers over the valley toward the encamped foe, Jonathan (the Prince) conceives an idea. "God is not limited," he declares. ". . . the Lord is not restrained to save by many or by few" (1 Samuel 14:6). The Philistines have indeed amassed a mighty army—but God is mightier than the enemy hosts. Forthwith Jonathan turns to the young man whom he has appointed to carry his armor. "Come," says the Prince of Israel, "let us cross over to the garrison of these uncircumcised . . . the Lord will work for us" (1 Samuel 14:6).

Approaching enemy territory, the men hear the shouted challenge from the Philistine garrison: "Come up to us and we will tell you something" (1 Samuel 14:12). Jonathan perceives this as an indication of the will of God to proceed. Moving right into the face of the foe, the man of God en-counters the forwardmost elements deployed on the enemy battle line and, with the assistance of the young armor bearer, slays about twenty Philistines. Timely as are all the acts of God, a mighty earthquake occurs now under the very feet of the invading troops. ". . . the earth quaked, so that it became a great trembling" (1 Samuel 14:15).

In the confusion which follows, "every man's sword" is turned "against his fellow" (1 Samuel 14:20) and, without any further action on the part of Jonathan, "the multitude" of the Philistines "melted away; and they went here and there" (1 Samuel 14:16). The inspired record draws the curtain on this crucial event in the experience of Israel with these appropriate words: "So the Lord delivered Israel that day" (1 Samuel 14:23).

Almost three thousand years have passed into history since that fateful event in Israel, yet the world has changed but little. We possess a technology unknown to the combatants of Geba and Michmash, but the heart of man is as evil today as ever in the long past. And beset as he is with enemy forces on every hand, those on whose shoulders the burdens of the nation rest readily lose their morale, tremble at the over-whelming odds, and retreat eastward over the Jordan to safety. We are living in the era of the dropout Christian. An example of this is a dear retired pastor who wrote us recently, "You can't beat the devil. No use trying to remove tempta-tion. Pornography and immorality will always be pushed on television. You might as well quit fighting it."

Almost without realizing it, the average Christian in our time has given up the fight. Content to go to church, live a decent life, and mind his own business, he concerns himself little with his local precinct, the proceedings at City Hall and the great issues confronting the nation. The field of battle has been abandoned largely to the forces of human-ism, secularism, and socialism, which have mounted a three-pronged thrust against the jugular of our trembling society. Christians retreat to secret caves, cellars, and pits for prayer, fellowship, and Bible study, contenting themselves with the exercise of piety while the enemy plunders the land at will. The luxuries of the spirit have become ends in themselves. The day of battle has come—but few there are to fight.

This is the day for a new Jonathan. His approach to the humanly impossible problem of his time is packed with meaning for the Christian today. First, he assessed the situation accurately. He knew precisely what the odds were. Second, he recognized that the time for action was at hand. The record does not convey any hint of a special service of worship or prayer. Jonathan felt as Dwight L. Moody did when the ship on which he was a passenger caught fire and the great evangelist declared, "I belong to the bucket brigade." In the third place, Jonathan placed complete confidence in God, but he did not allow his faith in God's power to dampen his personal zeal for action. Finally, Jonathan moved straight into action with all his might. "Come," he said to the young man at his side, "let us cross over to the garrison of these uncircumcised . . . ."

The Philistine stranglehold on America can be broken. Moral decay can be arrested. Corruption in government, dishonesty in the media, immorality in the theater, secularism, hedonism and existentialism in education, robbery of our people through inflation—these and a host of related ills can be treated effectively through the power of God. The pagan Philistine in our midst can be routed. All that is needed is a small remnant of stouthearted Christians who, like Jonathan, will assess the situation, recognize the opportunity, place confidence in God and cross over to do battle with the enemy.

Finally, be strong in the Lord, and in the strength of His might.

Put on the full armor of God, that you may be able to stand firm against the schemes of the devil.

For our struggle is not against flesh and blood, but against the rulers, against the powers, against the world forces of this darkness, against the spiritual forces of wickedness in the heavenly places.

Therefore, take up the full armor of God, that you may be able to resist in the evil day, and having done everything, to stand firm.

Ephesians 6:10–13